FIVE

SPEAKI
FATHER'S
BLESSING

52 Blessings and 365 Promises
To Speak Over Your Children

NEIL KENNEDY

SPEAKING THE FATHER'S BLESSING
ISBN

Copyright © 2014
FivestarMan
402B W. Mount Vernon St., Box 333
Nixa, MO 65714

Editor: Linda A. Schantz
Cover Design: Peppermedia, LLC

DEDICATION

I dedicate this book to my three children and their spouses:
Alexandra and Aric Schauer
Chase and Ari Kennedy
Courtney and Jordan Weston
and to their children.

I live with one goal in mind —
to hear my children tell their children,

"We serve the God of my father."

TABLE OF CONTENTS

★ ★ ★ ★ ★

SECTION ONE

★ ★ ★ ★ ★

SECTION TWO

SPEAKING THE
FATHER'S
BLESSING

★ ★ ★ ★ ★

SECTION
ONE

CHAPTER ONE

FATHER ABRAHAM

He is called the Father of many nations. His descendants are numerous. Three religious groups — Jewish, Muslim, and Christian — trace their spiritual lineage directly to him.

Who was this man? What distinguished him from other men? What was so special about the man called Abram that would catch the attention of God, causing Him to rename him Abraham?

It's amazing to think about being *the man* God selected to impart His blessing to and establish an everlasting covenant with you and your descendants forever.

On the surface of things, you might say he was very ordinary. Abraham was the eldest son of Terah, a Bedouin from Ur of the Chaldeans. Terah's goal was to move his family to Canaan and establish a legacy; however, experiencing the tragic loss in the premature death of his third son, Haran, Terah's journey was cut short. When Terah and his family members arrived in the city named Haran,

Terah could go no further. What should have been a short stop became a permanent memorial for Terah and his abandoned dreams.

Then *the Voice,* the clear and specific voice of God, spoke directly to Abraham to leave everything — his security, his inheritance, his father's household — to travel to an unknown destination.

You would have to be pretty confident in your ability to hear and distinguish the voice of God if you were willing to leave everything and go... to simply start moving in an uncharted direction! Yet, that's exactly what Abraham did.

> *By faith Abraham, when called to go to a place he would later receive as his inheritance, obeyed and went, even though he did not know where he was going. By faith he made his home in the promised land like a stranger in a foreign country; he lived in tents, as did Isaac and Jacob, who were heirs with him of the same promise.*
>
> *Hebrews 11:8, 9 NIV*

In order for God to establish a covenant with him, Abraham would need a new territory, a new dream, a new way of going and doing. But the promise wasn't just for Abraham. The promise was also for Abraham's descendants who would follow his path, not just geographically, but also in the steps God had directed him to take as a father.

To establish a covenant that would last, God needed a man who had enough faith to believe for something that would require more than his lifetime to achieve.

ABRAHAM WAS CHOSEN BECAUSE GOD TRUSTED HIM IN HIS FATHERHOOD

> *For I know him, that he will command his children and his household after him, and they shall keep the way of the Lord, to do justice and judgment; that the Lord may bring upon Abraham that which he hath spoken of him.*
>
> *Genesis 18:19 KJV*

Abraham was selected from all other men to be the recipient of the everlasting covenant because God knew Abraham would direct his children. He knew Abraham would disciple and discipline his children, bringing them up with intentional direction.

Direct your children onto the right path, and when they are older, they will not leave it.

Proverbs 22:6 NLT

God's everlasting covenant with a man requires that man to skillfully and faithfully pass on the provisions of the covenant; otherwise, the promise would die with one unfaithful generation.

God is selective. He looks within the heart of a man to make His choice. Something resided within Abraham that got the attention of God. It was Abraham's unwavering desire to be a father.

Fathering is more than having children. Fathering is **raising** children. It's directing them. It's imprinting your vision and values upon them. It's investing your influence into their lives.

So now, my sons, listen to me. Never stray from what I am about to say.

Proverbs 5:7 NLT

There is no greater influence in the lives of your children than the words you speak over them. **The blessing of the father is incredibly potent and powerful.** Your words give your children potential. As their father, you are prophesying their future!

God said, "I trust Abraham with my covenant because he directs his household well. He will keep order. He will instruct his children, and in doing so, he will secure the promise."

This is the foundation of fatherhood: The desire and ability to give intentional direction to your children, establishing vision and values for their lives, guaranteeing your progeny will be established upon the earth in righteousness.

By speaking and praying over your children, you set a course for them in life. You direct them in the way they should go. In disciplining them, you set their feet on a path to the future in the hope that when they are older they won't depart from it.

Don't think you won't face opposition. On the contrary, everything of value is challenged. This culture is going to resist everything you are speaking and praying over your child, but know that the words you speak and the prayers you pray will be effective and will not return void. Your words will accomplish the purpose for which you spoke them.

The tongue can bring death or life; those who love to talk will reap the consequences.

Proverbs 18:21 NLT

Father, you cannot underestimate the potential of the words that you speak over your children.

I remember the horrific moment when I witnessed a father make a derogatory remark to his daughter. I couldn't believe it. It was one of those defining moments that you are very sure you will never forget. The young lady was in the awkward phase of her pre-teenage years. As she was cutting a piece of pie, he looked at her and said, "I think you've had enough."

I saw the embarrassed and embittered look on his daughter's face. I'm certain he didn't weigh the repercussions his comment would have on her; however, his words caused a deep wound that penetrated her soul. From that very moment, she began to struggle with her body image. A sense of dysmorphia gripped her thinking. The anger that boiled her emotions became volatile. The aftereffects of this one tragic moment began a lifelong struggle for this young woman.

CHAPTER TWO

TEACH YOUR CHILDREN WELL

As a father, your words have the power of life and death. Solomon said, *"A wise man's heart guides his mouth, and his lips promote instruction"* (Proverbs 16:23). Rather than spewing out insults, a father should speak instruction.

This doesn't mean you can't expect excellence. On the contrary, your pursuit of excellence is what guards your mouth.

Many fathers make the fundamental mistake of assuming their children know what **they** know. At times we forget what it was like to learn what now seems obvious. **People don't know what they don't know.**

Teach your children the principles of life. Show them the way to live. Instruct them in the duties they should perform.

Moses was given the seemingly insurmountable task of leading an entire nation out of the bondage of slavery and into a promised life of freedom. Moses received a download of information and revelation from God. God instructed Moses in great detail about His character, His ways, and His precepts.

Each day, Moses sat in front of a crowd of complainers motivated by ignorance. They simply didn't know how to live in freedom. For generations they were slaves, but suddenly the people found themselves facing the struggles of liberty and personal responsibility. Moses had the task to lead them into making right decisions concerning the matters of life. He was the only one in the crowd who had direct revelation knowledge from God.

This posed a real problem. People spent hours, sometimes days, waiting their turn to receive answers to their questions.

Moses' father-in-law, Jethro, saw the overwhelming responsibility placed upon Moses. He witnessed the frustration in the camp. He knew something had to be done, so he proposed a solution.

> Moses' father-in-law said to him, "What you are doing is not good. You and the people with you will certainly wear yourselves out, for the thing is too heavy for you. You are not able to do it alone. Now obey my voice; I will give you advice, and God be with you! You shall represent the people before God and bring their cases to God, and you shall warn them about the statutes and the laws, and make them know the way in which they must walk and what they must do. Moreover, look for able men from all the people, men who fear God, who are trustworthy and hate a bribe, and place such men over the people as chiefs of thousands, of hundreds, of fifties, and of tens. And let them judge the people at all times. Every great matter they shall bring to you, but any small matter they shall decide themselves. So it will be easier for you, and they will bear the burden with you. If you do this, God will direct you, you will be able to endure, and all this people also will go to their place in peace."
>
> *Exodus 18:17-23 ESV*

Jethro's advice is so foundational to leadership that businesses and corporations should take note. As men and fathers, we should certainly listen to this wise father-in-law's advice.

We should teach the *ways* and the *whys* of doing things to our children.

When you teach your children to make their beds, show them the tricks of tucking the sheets, folding the covers, and fluffing the pillows; but more importantly teach them that no one is assigned to make their beds but themselves. Teach them that making their beds creates order in their lives. Teach them that it's good stewardship to take care of their possessions. Teach them that order is what separates us from chaos.

Teach your son how to change the tire on a car and how to service and maintain an engine. Teach your children how to balance a checkbook. Teach them how to mow a yard and to respect property. Teach your son how to shake a man's hand with a firm grip.

Don't assume your children know what you know. Teach your children to come to you when they're facing a challenge they have never faced before. And when they do, make eye contact and listen to the entire issue. Listen, contemplate, and respond with an answer and a lesson on why you think your idea is the best approach.

Teach your children the way wisdom works, so they will not just learn the immediate answer, but they will also learn **the process** of making wise decisions. This is more important than just getting to the facts, because situations and circumstances are conditional, but principles are everlasting.

DESCEND INTO GREATNESS

In your relationships with one another, have the same mindset as Christ Jesus: Who, being in very nature God, did not consider equality with God something to be used to his own advantage; rather, he made himself nothing by taking the very nature of a servant, being made in human likeness. And being found in appearance as a man, he humbled himself by becoming obedient to death — even death on a cross!
                                    Philippians 2:5-8 NIV

Jesus descended from His position of equality with God to make eye contact with mankind.

We sometimes forget the perspective that we are always looking down at our children and they are always looking up to us. Kneel down to make eye contact. Descending to their level will help you relate to each other better.

Descending is not only humbling but it is also exalting. When you lower yourself, you lift your child up. Your descent helps build up your child's confidence to look you in the eye.

You have stooped to make me great.

Psalm 18:35 NCV

You never look taller as a man when you stoop down to look into the eyes of a child.

NEVER DISCIPLINE SOMEONE YOU HAVE NOT DISCIPLED

If you discipline your children without clear instruction you will cause them to have confusion. A lesson will not be learned if a child doesn't understand the **why** of the discipline.

My son did something foolish, so I sent him to his room to await his discipline. I was about to discipline him when I asked myself a question, "Did you teach him this was wrong and why it was wrong?"

Even though it seemed to be obvious that what he did was wrong, I had never taught him it was. I paused long enough to ask him, "Did you **know** this was wrong?" He responded with the usual, "Ugh, I don't know." I spent some time teaching him the principle he had broken. This teaching did much more than the pain of discipline would have ever done.

Never discipline someone you have not discipled.

DON'T LET TRUTH AND GRACE FORSAKE ONE ANOTHER

Mercy and truth have met together.

Psalm 85:10 NKJV

It takes a balance of truth and grace to raise a child. If you raise your child with only truth (or your laws), they will never live up to your rules or expectations. No one can fulfill all of the law. On the other hand, if you only give grace to your children, they will run wild without restraint. At times you must discipline. If you fail to do so, society will become their disciplinarian, and society has no mercy. Discipline is always best served by a legitimate authority in your child's life.

> *It is for discipline that you have to endure. God is treating you as sons. For what son is there whom his father does not discipline? If you are left without discipline, in which all have participated, then you are illegitimate children and not sons. Besides this, we have had earthly fathers who disciplined us and we respected them....*
>
> *Hebrews 12:7-9 ESV*

Discipline is actually a demonstration of legitimacy. In the end, your son or daughter will interpret it as an act of love, not meanness. Of course, they won't think it's pleasant at the time, but discipline produces lasting results.

By the way, don't tell your child the discipline is going to hurt you more than it hurts them. Tell them the truth, "This is going to hurt you. You won't want this to happen again."

I realize that we're living in a culture that doesn't have a clue as to how to administer discipline appropriately. This is clearly evidenced in the unrestrained behavior of young people today.

I recall another time my son did something deserving of punishment; however, this time it was purely out of disobedience not ignorance. I needed to discipline him. As I was approaching him to discipline him, I made the statement, "Son, you know that this was wrong, don't you?"

"Yes," he responded.

"Do you know you deserve this discipline?" I asked.

He acknowledged that he did.

At that moment I realized I had a great opportunity to teach the lesson of grace. I shared with my son how grace works. I explained we receive grace, not because we deserve it, but we receive grace when we don't deserve it. I taught him punishment still had to be administered for sin, but someone else took the punishment to spare us the shame and pain of our wrongdoing.

Then I told him I would extend this undeserved grace to him, and I would pay the price for his disobedience.

He received the lesson well.

CHAPTER THREE

DISCIPLINE IS DISCIPLESHIP

The purpose behind discipline is to teach. It shouldn't be just punitive. If we fail to teach the lesson of why they are being disciplined, punishing our children will only cause confusion. Many children have run away from homes or secluded themselves in their rooms, because they haven't properly interpreted the hardness of their fathers as an act of love.

Never discipline until you are in control. Don't fly off the handle. Don't loose your temper. Too many fathers have horrific stories of losing control of their anger and causing irreparable harm to their relationships.

The point of discipline is to train your child to control their behavior and emotions. If you aren't in control of your own, the lesson is lost in translation.

Waiting often makes the punishment more powerful. Let them simmer while they're waiting — no phone, no computer, no television, no games — just four walls and their thoughts. Then when the discipline occurs, the lesson will be received.

Don't count to three. How many times have you been in the checkout line of a store when you've seen an exasperated mother with an unruly child? As the mother attempts to exercise her command over the situation, it becomes obvious the child is in control. "Mommy is going to count to three...."

In the history of parenting this has never worked. Counting to three, five or ten only teaches your child delayed obedience. Delayed obedience is disobedience.

There will be events in your child's life when he or she will need a reactionary response to your words. Hesitation could put him or her in danger.

There is a lesson in the movie, *"Man on Fire,"* when John Creasy, the former secret-ops man turned bodyguard, is teaching Pita to explode off the blocks for an upcoming swim met. He teaches his naive protégé not to hesitate when she hears the clap of his hands. The lesson comes into play not only for swimming, but also when she is about to be kidnapped. The explosion of gunfire reflexively sends her spontaneously running.

As a father, you don't want to instill fear with your voice to protect your child. You want to inspire obedience — obedience to recognize, understand, and immediately respond to your voice.

Teaching and discipline are fundamental to your children hearing your words. Discipline is the gatekeeper to promise.

If your children can't trust your disciplines, they will never believe your promises. Abraham was selected to carry the promises of the covenant and entrust those promises to his children and to their children.

A good man leaves an inheritance to his children's children.
Proverbs 13:22a ESV

In order to guarantee this inheritance, Abraham guarded his household well.

PROTECT THE ATMOSPHERE OF YOUR HOME

The time came for the son of the promise, Isaac, to be weaned from his mother. It was an important rite of passage for a young child. During the feast celebrating the occasion, Ishmael began to mock his half-brother. Sarah saw it and realized that if Ishmael were allowed to stay in the household, strife between the boys would destroy the covenant.

Strife is an evil that cannot be tolerated in the home.

Where jealousy and selfish ambition exist, there will be disorder and every vile practice.

James 3:16 ESV

Sarah approached Abraham about the matter, and although Abraham knew the danger of mockery, he was concerned about what would happen to Ishmael outside of their home. But God reassured Abraham that Sarah was right. Ishmael had to go. In order for the covenant of blessing to flourish in his family, it would need a protective environment.

There is a great lesson in this story for those who have blended families. It is very difficult to raise children, especially if they are stepchildren. You must value the atmosphere of peace. Don't underestimate the destructive power of strife.

I am not suggesting that we should drive out every disobedient child from our homes, nor am I recommending that you overreact to a bad attitude. I do believe, however, that you must protect your home from the vileness of rebellion.

I grew up in a strife-filled home. Alcohol abuse, drug abuse, and the haze of cigarette smoke drifted in the rooms. Loud and obnoxious curse words and constant bickering were the norm. I found myself retreating to my room for a reprieve, and as soon as possible I looked for my escape. I was determined not to allow that kind of environment in my household.

Our home has always been a peaceful home. My wife worked diligently to keep it clean and in order, even when our children were small. But more importantly, we worked very hard to keep strife out. Our children's friends would visit our house and inevitably comment on how peaceful our home was. We valued that because we wanted our children to feel comfortable bringing their friends to the house.

ABRAHAM BELIEVED THE PROMISE WITHOUT WAVERING

By faith Abraham, when he was tested...

Hebrews 11:17 ESV

Abraham received an instruction concerning Isaac that would have been extremely difficult to hear. The instruction was to take his son and offer him as a sacrifice. This was never asked before, nor was it ever repeated. This is the one and only time God asked for a human sacrifice.

This request seems so contrary to the character of God. It is contrary to God's nature. There was something else going on. This test was to ascertain the quality of Abraham's character, what he thought, his motivations, and how he would behave in this situation.

To understand, we must remember that God provided Isaac in the first place. God released the potential for Abraham to have an heir. The question was whether the gift God provided to Abraham was greater in Abraham's estimation than obedience to the Giver.

When Abraham and Isaac were ascending the mountain to worship, Isaac asked a good question: *"The fire and wood are here, but where is the lamb for the burnt offering?"* (Genesis 22:7)

Abraham's response reveals the deep confidence he had in the God who called him out of Haran to the promised inheritance. Abraham said, *"God himself will provide the lamb for the burnt offering, my son"* (Genesis 22:8).

Hebrews 11 gives insight into Abraham's thinking. It reveals in verse 19, *"Abraham reasoned that God could raise the dead."*

Abraham did not hesitate to make the offer because he reasoned on the character of God. He knew God was not a man that He could lie. God said it was through Isaac that the promise would be fulfilled, so Abraham believed that even if he sacrificed his son, Isaac would be raised from the dead.

There will be times you must put the promises of God above everything that appears to be dead.

In raising your children, you have a responsibility to believe God's promises and speak them out loud, declaring them for your children.

Abraham said, *"God himself will provide."* He declared his confidence in God's provision for the sacrifice. In doing so, he was prophetically speaking of the coming Messiah, the Savior of mankind, the Lamb slain before the foundation of the earth.

God needed a man to believe for the Messianic prophesy and declare it so effectively that within the heart of Abraham, he had already sacrificed his son. This was credited to Abraham as righteousness.

The promises you speak over your children can take on the weight of destiny. Your words matter. They are not trivial expressions. They mean something.

We must take our words seriously. They are empowered with life and death.

They are not just idle words for you — they are your life. By them you will live long in the land....

Deuteronomy 32:47 NIV

Don't brush this off.

We're living in a culture that spews out worthless words. Our society speaks boastful, snarky, ridiculous things. They mock, accuse, slander, and gossip. They lie at any convenience. They jest without honor. They're vile and impudent, and their profanity reveals an ignorance of the power of the spoken word.

The word for idle in the Hebrew is *"ràk,"* which means **empty, vain, impoverished, poor,** and/or **wicked.**

Words matter.

This book is about the words you speak as a father. It is about the powerful words that you pray over your children.

This is the confidence we have in approaching God: that if we ask anything according to his will, he hears us. And if we know that he hears us — whatever we ask — we know that we have what we asked of him.

1 John 5:14 NIV

You will never have confidence in your prayers if you fail to be prudent with your words.

John Osteen said, "You can change the whole course of your life by looking at the promises of God and daring to believe them."

Children need a confident father to lead them. I am not talking about a man who is arrogant and shows no meekness. Children need a man who knows how to be strong in the things of God, confident in the spiritual promises of HIs Word, and faithful to speak those promises with conviction.

As a father, don't try to draw your strength from your wife to lead your children. Go to God and draw your strength from Him, then turn and boldly say, *"Follow me, as I follow Christ."*

Too many men fail to lead their families, largely because they mistakenly believe that they are not spiritual. That's not true. You were created in the image of God; you are spiritual. You are not alone. In fact, nine out ten men say that they believe in God. *(Source: "Women Are The Backbone Of Christian Congregations In America," www.barna.org)*

As a man, you are also assigned the responsibility to teach spiritual things to your family. Don't try to pawn this off on the church or on your wife. You own this.

Husbands, love your wives, just as Christ loved the church and gave himself up for her to make her holy, cleansing her by the washing with water through the word, and to present her to himself as a radiant church, without stain or wrinkle or any other blemish, but holy and blameless. In the same way, husbands ought to love their wives as their own bodies. He who loves his wife loves himself.

Ephesians 5:25-28 NIV

Paul said that husbands should love their wives in the same way as Christ loved the Church. How? By speaking his words over her, which cleanses her, presenting back to him a beautiful and pure woman, without stains, wrinkles, or blemishes.

We've pawned off enough of our responsibilities, we need to take the promise of God seriously and use our words to benefit our families.

CHAPTER FOUR

IMPRESS YOUR CHILDREN

These commandments that I give you today are to be on your hearts. Impress them on your children. Talk about them when you sit at home and when you walk along the road, when you lie down and when you get up. Tie them as symbols on your hands and bind them on your foreheads. Write them on the doorframes of your houses and on your gates.

Deuteronomy 6:6-9 NIV

To impress means **to sharpen; to teach; to be pierced.** To impress something upon someone means **to speak sharp statements to them with the intention that they will be quickly remembered and obeyed.** The idea of impressing your children is to make a distinguishable mark upon them. It means **to inculcate or repetitively drill into the mind.**

Children have a way of remembering our mantras — those pithy statements we make that have substance. It's always a great acknowledgement when someone quotes something I have said or have written, but nothing compares to hearing my children repeat something I've said. Wow! I love it when that happens.

Did you notice that *to impress* also means *to pierce?* Could it be possible that one of the byproducts of a lack of parental teaching is that young people are mutilating their bodies with piercings? They may be so desperate to be impressed by someone or something that they will readily tattoo pictures, phrases, or symbolic images upon themselves. Alternately, they may have something to say but they don't know how to express it, so they cut and mark themselves in an effort to get attention and to be heard. In either case, this could be a direct byproduct of the absence of a patriarchal influence.

Rather than allow society to mark them, here's how we can make an indelible impression upon our children with the Word of God:

1. **Make it a part of the conversation in your household.**

    This should be a daily pattern but not in a fake, religious sense. It should just be part of the conversation during normal routines.

    For an example, talk about something that is making the headlines in the news. How does it relate to the principles of God's Word? If someone is involved in a scandal, what led to it? A sexual sin? A lack of integrity in politics or business? What scriptural example could be used to explain it?

    When you're working in the yard, can you teach a work ethic that corresponds to our responsibilities to rule the earth, such as taking authority over our property? What happens if we don't cultivate the yard? What about the house? Do we keep it maintained? Are we good stewards of what God has given us?

    What about what we watch on television? Are we entertained by something we wouldn't allow in our lives in any other circumstance? Do we watch people make out in front of us? Are we entertained by murder? Do we eat while people are being dissected in front of us?

2. **As you're traveling**

I really took advantage of this with my family. Drive time became teaching time for me. When we got in my SUV to go somewhere, I would begin to teach about principles in the Bible. Our family had the best dialogue while we traveled.

I believe God relates to us in the daily commute. As we go, God speaks to us. Adam walked with God in the cool of the day. Enoch walked with God, and he was no more for God took him. Noah walked with God as a righteous man during a wicked generation. Abraham's steps were ordered as he walked to inherit a new land. Moses walked barefooted on a mountain as he received revelation from God. When Jesus came to earth, He, too, walked with man.

As you're traveling, spend time conversing with your family.

3. **Before you go to sleep**

Bedtime is a vital time to impress upon your children the things of God.

When my children were young, I made it a habit to tuck them into bed each night. I would tell them faith stories that I would make up, where the main character in the story was their age and gender so they could relate. I would make up situations where a belief in a principle from God's Word would help get them through a challenge.

Then I would speak a prayer over them for their sleep to be sweet, asking the Holy Spirit to instruct them during the night.

If you lie down, you will not be afraid; when you lie down, your sleep will be sweet.

Proverbs 3:24 ESV

4. **When you get up**

Starting the day off with instruction and motivation is a key to training children to take action in their lives. When they get up it's the perfect time to make goals and forecast the day. Help your child with a "To Do" list. An assignment gives your child purpose and creates order for them.

Where there is no revelation, people cast off restraint; but blessed is the one who heeds wisdom's instruction.
                                                    Proverbs 29:18 NIV

The Hebrew word for revelation is **"chazown,"** which means, **a vision concerning future events, or an oracle.** An oracle is often referred to as a person with whom God speaks. It refers to an authoritative and wise person who answers looming questions. You have the ability to answer questions and the responsibility to forecast your child's future for them with your words.

This is a weighty issue. Very few fathers take this responsibility seriously. But those who do will see amazing results in their children's lives.

"I am a byproduct of my father's search for greatness in a small town." — Nick Saban, Jr., Head Football Coach, University of Alabama

Children without a vision, or a revelation concerning the future — those who do not have answers — stumble all over themselves. Without this guiding instruction they cast off restraint. They have no boundaries and no guiding principles for successful living.

Children who are raised with a pursuit toward a better future and a hope of things to come — those who have answers to the challenges of life — are motivated and guided with principles and purpose.

5. **Tie them as symbols on your hands.**

    Not long ago a small bracelet with the acronym WWJD became a huge success. Of course, WWJD stood for a question that really served as an answer, "What Would Jesus Do?" Those who wore the bracelet were reminded when they were facing a challenge or a question from the circumstances of their day that there was a higher standard to live up to.

We have bracelets with the phrase, *FivestarMan* and *Authentic Manhood* printed upon them. I regularly hear from men who wear the bracelets. They tell me how it reminds them of their purpose to live up to God's original intent for authentic manhood.

Not long ago I was returning from a speaking engagement in California. Sitting next to me on the plane was a businessman. I noticed that he frequently was looking toward my wrist at my *FivestarMan* bracelet. He asked, "What is a *FivestarMan*?"

I shared with him about our efforts and movement to resurrect authentic manhood. I explained the five passions of authentic manhood (an adventurous spirit, entrepreneurial drive, gallant relationships, faithful character, and philanthropic in cause). He admired the bracelet so much that I reached into my briefcase and gave him one. This simple bracelet became a symbol on my hand for authentic manhood.

When each of my daughters turned thirteen, I presented them with a ring to wear as a symbol of purity. I told them that these rings were really gifts to be given to their future husbands as tokens representing their purity for marriage. Each ring became a symbol upon their hands to remind them of their future.

I truly believe that children want to have your vision and values stamped upon them. Remember, **to impress** means **to make a distinguishing mark upon them.**

6. Bind them upon their foreheads.

It is a Jewish tradition for men to wear the **"Tefillin"** or *phylacteries*, which are small, wooden, square boxes placed upon the forehead which house four scriptures:

And it shall be to you as a sign on your hand and as a memorial between your eyes, that the law of the Lord may be in your mouth. For with a strong hand the Lord has brought you out of Egypt.

Exodus 13:9 ESV

It shall be as a mark on your hand or frontlets between your eyes, for by a strong hand the Lord brought us out of Egypt.

Exodus 13:16 ESV

Tie them as symbols on your hands and bind them on your foreheads.

Deuteronomy 6:8 NIV

Fix these words of mine in your hearts and minds; tie them as symbols on your hands and bind them on your foreheads.

Deuteronomy 11:18 NIV

When a phylactery is placed upon a man, a spoken blessing is announced, *"Blessed be the name of His glorious kingdom forever and ever."*

Unfortunately, in many cases the purpose of these symbols have become confused and they are seen as some type of "magical" amulet to protect a person from evil. (When people attach a magical equation to a spiritual principle they pervert its power and compromise its meaning.)

We should take the more appropriate lesson to use these symbolic reminders that God is the protector of our children. He delivers His people out of bondage, and His hand will continue to guide our children's lives.

Our children need more than a rabbit's foot or a lucky charm; they need the reality of God's protection.

It's important that you build your child's confidence with faith for a blessed future through the God who watches over His Word to perform it.

7. **Write them upon your doorframes and the gates of your home.**

As a man, you are the gate of authority to your home. The gate that you open up is the gate others walk through. This can be good or bad. To access your home, people and things must come through you.

When Jesus cast out demons, religious leaders accused Jesus of using Beelzebub, the prince of demons. Their vile accusation was that Jesus used witchcraft to entice or manipulate others to become His followers.

Religious leaders were not fearful to use schemes in the form of questions to implant false accusations against Jesus. This was a normal tactic for them. Their questions were never designed to be informed or to receive answers. They were designed to plant false narratives. In reality, these leaders used manipulation to entice people to follow them rather than the truth.

This insidious plot backfired on them as Jesus exposed a principle the enemy often uses to take the possessions of a household.

If a house is divided against itself, that house cannot stand.
Mark 3:25 NIV

Division brings destruction. A house can withstand all kinds of destructive efforts and opposition, but it cannot endure an internal fraction.

Then Jesus added this amazing insight, *"No one can enter a strong man's house and plunder his goods, unless he first binds the strong man. Then indeed he may plunder his house"* (Mark 3:27 ESV).

The nemesis of man knows this principle and thereby schemes to bind us so that he can get possession of everything we hold valuable.

Everything we cherish is at stake. In order to protect the valuables in our homes, our families and possessions, we must guard the gate and keep our doors secure.

Proverbs 31 is often used for women as a guide for their lives, but the sacred wisdom of the Book of Proverbs is actually instructional wisdom of a father writing to his son. Proverbs 31 tells the son about the kind of woman he should search for and marry. It says, *"She watches over the affairs of her household"* (Proverbs 31:27).

The partnership of the man and woman to build their home is inseparable. Their complementary designs help build a hedge of protection that is difficult for the enemy to penetrate.

...If two of you on earth agree about anything they ask for, it will be done for them by my Father in heaven.

Matthew 18:19 NIV

There is nothing that has more potential than a covenant agreement of a husband and wife.

Establish the boundaries of your household with the Word of God. To do so, you will need to guard the voices that have access to your home.

JUST BECAUSE SOMEONE HAS A VOICE, IT DOESN'T MEAN THEY SHOULD BE HEARD

When satan possessed a serpent, he spoke to Eve and deceived her by his crafty argument, convincing her that disobedience to God's Word would not bring a penalty.

The Bible is clear: Eve was deceived but Adam **willingly** disobeyed God's command. Adam did not live up to his responsibility. He shouldn't have allowed the voice of a creep to speak to his wife, especially about spiritual matters!

When God made Adam, He gave him dominion over everything upon the earth. Adam should have stomped his foot on the devil.

As a father, you must establish your voice as one that is trusted, confident, and articulate in the things of God. Your voice is vital. Don't underestimate the influence your voice has in the life of your child. You must filter the voices that speak into your home: television, Internet, mobile phones, other people, etc. Don't allow anything to influence your home that doesn't align with Scripture.

It is vitally important that you and your wife walk in agreement concerning raising your children. Your wife's voice should be an echo of yours. You should speak the same language.

Every child attempts at some point to pit one parent against the other. It's a diversion tactic. If a child can play off of the sympathies of one parent against the harshness of another, he wins by getting the parents to focus on each other and not on the real issue of discipline.

The promise of impressing God's plan upon your children brings a huge guarantee with it. It's one that many parents find themselves confessing through traumatic periods or stages of rebellion.

Train up a child in the way he should go; even when he is old he will not depart from it.

Proverbs 22:6 ESV

The Hebrew word for train is, **"chanak,"** meaning, **to narrow.** You must narrow the direction for your child. You must take away options and establish boundaries. Children need to know where the limits are, and they will regularly test their boundaries.

We've all seen a young child who is wandering away from their parent but keeps looking back to see if their actions are being noticed. He will call back, "Mom (or Dad), do you see me?" The parent acknowledges, "Yes, honey, I can see you." This exercise usually continues until the moment the parent orders a retreat to their watchful safety. The boundary has been set.

When a child wanders, he will keep going until a parental voice of authority says, "Enough! Get back here!"

Training is for narrowing the focus and establishing boundaries.

The word for **train** in Proverbs 22:6 also means **to put something into the mouth to be tasted**. That's what we do as parents. We give our children tastes. We say, "Here, this is something that you will like. It's good for you. Try it." We also warn them from our life experiences, "This is poison. Don't taste it."

In the Middle Ages kings had butlers who tasted their food before it was served to make sure no poison had been slipped into it by a malevolent enemy. Parents are the taste-testers for their children. We preview the lessons and trials of life to spare our children by giving them wisdom we've learned before them. We've tasted it, tried it, and approved what they receive, so we can confidently say, this is good.

Now that you have tasted that the Lord is good...
1 Peter 2:3 NIV

Training your children is so much more than simply giving **rules** to follow. It's really giving **faith** to follow. Training empowers your children. It doesn't restrict them. It protects your children. It doesn't expose them to harm.

One of the gravest mistakes within the church culture is to train what we shouldn't do and what we shouldn't believe. Rather, we should raise our children with what we **should** believe and what we **should** do. We're not enforcing "Christianized" behavior; we're training righteous thinking versus unrighteous thinking — wisdom versus foolishness — knowledge versus ignorance — blessing versus a curse.

CHAPTER FIVE

THE BLESSING OF A FATHER

There are two ways to gain wisdom: by a mentor or through pain. I recommend finding a mentor.

Now that we know how valuable our voice is as fathers, we must learn what we should say and how to say it.

This book is a tool chest you can draw upon while you're raising your children. It includes 52 blessings you can speak over your children. Each of the blessings are explained and expressed through a simple process: **precept, principle, practice, profession,** and supporting **promises**. This process will help us communicate the blessing and make it a powerful tool in raising our children.

PRECEPT

You have commanded your precepts to be kept diligently.
Psalm 119:4 ESV

A **precept** is **a spoken commandment or rule for order; a divine oracle to prescribe wisdom**. Precepts are guideposts for a journey.

We're blessed with the ability to read the Bible and apply its ancient wisdom to practical applications for our lives and for the benefit of our children.

Precepts come with an enormous amount of authority because they are the oracles of God given to men. Using them as a guide for wise living brings that authority into our lives.

Oh that my ways may be established to keep Your statutes!
Psalm 119:5 NASB

A precept helps establish the course of life, the moral character, and daily habits your children should have. In other words, precepts prosper you. To prosper means your journey will go well with you (Ephesians 6:3). You want your children's lives to be full and rich and large, but you will need to give them the wisdom to get there.

- Understanding precepts helps your children understand God's character and His actions (Psalm 119:15).

- Knowing the precepts will preserve your children's lives (Psalm 119:40).

- Living by the precepts will give your children liberty and freedom (Psalm 119:45).

- Precepts will establish good habits (Psalm 119:56).

- By knowing the precepts of God your children will choose the right friends (Psalm 119:63).

- Precepts will guard your children from peer pressure (Psalm 119:69).

- Knowing precepts will mature your children well beyond their age (Psalm 119:100).

- Precepts will direct the steps of your children, helping them make good choices (Psalm 119:104).

- Knowing the precepts of God will keep your children from injury and harm (Psalm 119:134).

- God will save, protect, and promote your children because they live by God's precepts (Psalm 119:173).

The precepts of God bring incredible benefits to your child's life, but you will need more than simply quoting them for your child to have the guaranteed results.

PRINCIPLE

We need to interpret the precepts into the principles behind them. Principles help us understand the inevitable results or consequences of precepts. Understanding the principle behind the precept helps us interpret it for universal application.

Let me give you an example:

The Bible says, *"Do not muzzle an ox while it is treading out the grain"* (Deuteronomy 25:4 NIV). This is a precept established to govern the conduct of people while an ox is working in the field. Few of us own an ox, though, so on the surface it would seem this precept is not applicable to us. But the principle behind this precept is that a laborer should receive nourishment from his labor. The Apostle Paul used this precept and principle to encourage the Church regarding the financial support he was given from those who were the beneficiaries of his labor (1 Corinthians 9:9). Paul later applied it to ministerial compensation in the Church (1 Timothy 5:18).

The precept is the established **authority**. The principle behind it is the **interpretation** of the precept. The practice is the **application** of the principle into daily life.

PRACTICE

Putting principles into practice is what separates the wise from the foolish. It's not enough to hear the precepts. What's important is to apply them into our lives and impress them upon our children.

Champions do daily what average men do occasionally.

One of the real efforts of raising children is establishing habits that benefit them. Brushing their teeth, taking baths, eating a balanced diet, exercise, reading, picking up after themselves — these are all great habits to teach your children.

Whatever you have learned or received or heard from me, or seen in me — put it into practice....

Philippians 4:9 NIV

That is what we're doing with the **precept-principle-practice** of Scripture. We're establishing exercises that govern our lives and bring us great benefits.

This has been my practice: I obey your precepts.

Psalm 119:56 NIV

Teaching our children to practice what we've taught them is vital for their success. We're not just hearing the Word; we're doing it, practicing it, and seeing the results of it in our lives.

PROFESSION

A **profession** is **to declare openly, to speak out, to concede or to promise**. It is also a principal calling in life, as in **your profession.**

We are not only people of **confession**, but we are also people of **profession**. To understand the difference, a confession is to admit a wrong, while a profession is to declare a right.

The conception of a Christian, the moment when someone truly becomes a follower of Christ, happens at the time of a profession of faith.

..."The word is near you; it is in your mouth and in your heart," that is, the message concerning faith that we proclaim: If you declare with your mouth, "Jesus is Lord," and believe in your heart that God raised him from the dead, you will be saved. For it is with your heart that you believe and are justified, and it is with your mouth that you profess your faith and are saved.

Romans 10:8-10 NIV

The process of a profession is hearing, believing, and speaking. We use the **precept-principle-practice** to believe, and the **profession-promises** to declare them into our lives and the lives of our children.

We see a **precept** in Scripture, interpret the **principle** behind it, make its application into a **practice**, then **profess** it into our lives. Our profession is a spoken statement of our belief. It is faith expressed verbally.

A profession is a prayer, not only a private one, but also a public one. You speak a profession based upon the knowledge of the *precept-principle-practice*. As you make a faith-filled profession, it empowers and gives you a sense of confidence in your belief that your children will receive its benefits.

PROMISES

Each of the 52 blessings in this book includes promises from Scripture to correspond with the profession of faith that you declare. Speak these promises daily in agreement with the weekly blessing upon your children.

Remember: Champions do daily what average men do occasionally. Make speaking a blessing over your children a daily habit. Establishing good habits is a powerful tool in the lives of great men.

Even Jesus had habits. He had a habit of attending synagogue.

He went to Nazareth, where he had been brought up, and on the Sabbath day he went into the synagogue, as was his custom. He stood up to read....

Luke 4:16 NIV

The Psalmist had a habit of praying seven times.

Seven times a day I praise you for your righteous laws.

Psalm 119:164 NIV

Daniel, a man who is described as having an excellent spirit, had a habit of praying three times each day.

Now when Daniel learned that the decree had been published, he went home to his upstairs room where the windows opened toward Jerusalem. Three times a day he got down on his knees and prayed, giving thanks to his God, just as he had done before.

Daniel 6:10 NIV

Speaking The Father's Blessing is a tool for you to keep handy. Keep it with you so you can take time to speak out the promises of God over your children on a daily basis.

This will be a game changer in your children's lives. You will see tremendous results in your family. It won't happen in a day, but it will happen over the course of time, if you are diligent with it.

SPEAKING THE
FATHER'S
BLESSING

★ ★ ★ ★ ★

SECTION
TWO

BLESSING ONE

INCREASE!

★ ★ ★ ★ ★

PRECEPT

Be fruitful and increase....

Genesis 1:28 NIV

PRINCIPLE

Within the spiritual DNA of man is the encoded promise to reproduce who we are and to increase upon the earth. As contrary as this is to modern culture, this is the blessing upon mankind. We are to populate the earth. In other words, God has made us to duplicate who we are and what we do exponentially upon the earth.

PRACTICE

You want to bless your children with this same blessing. Reproduction is inherent in who we are as His image-bearers upon the earth. We are reproducers. We recreate in our own likeness. We're the shadowed images of God. And our children, grandchildren, and prodigy shadow us upon the earth.

PROFESSION

"I speak the blessing over my children: 'Be fruitful and increase upon the earth.' The earth is my children's field to explore and cultivate. May God's original blessing be upon them. I bless my sons and daughters to increase."

PROMISES TO SPEAK THIS WEEK

1. *Then God blessed Noah and his sons, saying to them, "Be fruitful and increase in number and fill the earth." Genesis 9:1 NIV*

2. *May God Almighty bless you and make you fruitful and increase your numbers until you become a community of peoples. Genesis 28:3 NIV*

3. *God said to him, "I am God Almighty; be fruitful and increase in number." Genesis 35:11a NIV*

4. *"...I will make you fruitful and multiply you, and I will make of you a company of peoples and will give this land to your offspring after you for an everlasting possession." Genesis 48:4 ESV*

5. *I will look on you with favor and make you fruitful and increase your numbers, and I will keep my covenant with you. Leviticus 26:9 NIV*

6. *I myself will gather the remnant of my flock out of all the countries where I have driven them and will bring them back to their pasture, where they will be fruitful and increase in number. Jeremiah 23:3 NIV*

7. *I will increase the number of people and animals living on you, and they will be fruitful and become numerous. I will settle people on you as in the past and will make you prosper more than before. Then you will know that I am the Lord. Ezekiel 36:11 NIV*

NOTES

BLESSING TWO

UNDISTURBED COMPOSURE

PRECEPT

All your [spiritual] children shall be disciples [taught by the Lord and obedient to His will], and great shall be the peace and undisturbed composure of your children.

Isaiah 54:13 AMP

PRINCIPLE

The Lord is personally involved in teaching your children. In the midst of chaos, your children have a calm demeanor, undisturbed composure, and obedient behavior.

PRACTICE

You're not alone in wanting the best for your children. Jesus is also interested in making your children disciples of His teaching so they share in the blessing that comes from obedience: peace and undisturbed composure.

PROFESSION

"My children are taught by the Lord and great is their peace. They have obedient spirits and undisturbed composure in the midst of chaos."

PROMISES TO SPEAK THIS WEEK

1. *It is written in the Prophets: "They will all be taught by God." Everyone who has heard the Father and learned from him comes to me. John 6:45 NIV*

2. *And in your Seed [Christ] shall all the nations of the earth be blessed and [by Him] bless themselves, because you have heard and obeyed My voice. Genesis 22:18 AMP*

3. *You are the descendants (sons) of the prophets and the heirs of the covenant which God made and gave to your forefathers, saying to Abraham, And in your Seed (Heir) shall all the families of the earth be blessed and benefited. Acts 3:25 AMP*

4. *Your word is a lamp to my feet and a light to my path. Psalm 119:105 NKJV*

5. *So let us seize and hold fast and retain without wavering the hope we cherish and confess and our acknowledgement of it, for He Who promised is reliable (sure) and faithful to His word. Hebrews 10:23 AMP*

6. *The Lord will perfect that which concerns me; Your mercy, O Lord, endures forever; do not forsake the works of Your hands. Psalm 138:8 NKJV*

7. *Call unto me, and I will answer thee, and show thee great and mighty things, which thou knowest not. Jeremiah 33:3 KJV*

NOTES

I AM RAISING A HERO!

PRECEPT

Their children will be mighty in the land; the generation of the upright will be blessed.

Psalm 112:2 NIV

PRINCIPLE

The benefit of obedience is heroic children. Yes, heroic. The Hebrew word for **mighty** means **strong, mighty, and impetuous** or **conditioned to respond without wavering in thought.**

PRACTICE

You want your children to have the ability to make quick decisions. They need to have reflexive thinking regarding right and wrong. In handling temptation, people often give themselves time to reason it in their thinking. Eve considered the tree — that it was pleasing to the eye, had satisfying food, and might bring gain; however, three positives do not make it right when you are disobeying God's Word.

PROFESSION

"My children are heroic among their peers. They are quick to respond without hesitation to circumstances. They are strong."

PROMISES TO SPEAK THIS WEEK

1. *They will have no fear of bad news; their hearts are steadfast, trusting in the Lord. Psalm 112:7 NIV*

2. *Their hearts are secure, they will have no fear; in the end they will look in triumph on their foes. Psalm 112:8 NIV*

3. *There is no fear in love. But perfect love drives out fear, because fear has to do with punishment. The one who fears is not made perfect in love. 1 John 4:18 NIV*

4. *For everyone born of God overcomes the world. This is the victory that has overcome the world, even our faith. 1 John 5:4 NIV*

5. *I have strength for all things in Christ Who empowers me [I am ready for anything and equal to anything through Him Who infuses inner strength into me; I am self-sufficient in Christ's sufficiency]. Philippians 4:13 AMP*

6. *In all these things we are more than conquerors through him who loved us. Romans 8:37 NIV*

7. *I am convinced that neither death nor life, neither angels nor demons, neither the present nor the future, nor any powers, neither height nor depth, nor anything else in all creation, will be able to separate us from the love of God that is in Christ Jesus our Lord. Romans 8:38-39 NIV*

NOTES

_____

_____

_____

_____

_____

_____

_____

_____

_____

_____

_____

_____

_____

_____

_____

_____

_____

_____

_____

_____

_____

_____

_____

BLESSING FOUR

LIVE LONG
AND PROSPER

PRECEPT

*Children, obey your parents in the Lord,
for this is right. "Honor your father and
mother" — which is the first
commandment with a promise — "so
that it may go well with you and that
you may enjoy long life on the earth."*

Ephesians 6:1-3 NIV

PRINCIPLE

The benefit of showing honor is a long and prosperous life.

PRACTICE

Teaching your children to honor you is not self-serving; it is serving them a long and prosperous life. Honor is a protocol of authority. You serve under authority so you can manage what you are over. Life goes well for children who honor their parents. Those who do not show their parents honor face difficult consequences from society.

PROFESSION

"My children show me honor, guaranteeing them a prosperous and long life."

PROMISES TO SPEAK THIS WEEK

1. *"Honor your father and your mother, that your days may be long in the land that the Lord your God is giving you." Exodus 20:12 NKJV*

2. *"Honor your father and your mother, as the Lord your God has commanded you, so that you may live long and that it may go well with you in the land the Lord your God is giving you." Deuteronomy 5:16 NKJV*

3. *He has declared that he will set you in praise, fame and honor high above all the nations he has made and that you will be a people holy to the Lord your God, as he promised. Deuteronomy 26:19 NIV*

4. *Do not merely listen to the word, and so deceive yourselves. Do what it says. James 1:22 NIV*

5. *If any of you lacks wisdom, you should ask God, who gives generously to all without finding fault, and it will be given to you. James 1:5 NIV*

6. *…Those who honor me I will honor, but those who despise me will be disdained. 1 Samuel 2:30 NIV*

7. *…Whoever does not honor the Son does not honor the Father who sent him. John 5:23 ESV*

NOTES

BLESSING FIVE

PLANS AND PURPOSES

PRECEPT

"I know the plans I have for you,"
declares the Lord, "plans to
prosper you and not to harm you,
plans to give you hope
and a future."

Jeremiah 29:11 NIV

PRINCIPLE

God has planned a future for your children.

PRACTICE

You want your children to have an optimistic hope for their future. As children go through difficult seasons of change in their childhood they need to have a firm foundation, knowing that they have a bright future and hope. Having the assurance that comes from God's plan for them will strengthen their resolve and fend off depression and other trappings of youth.

PROFESSION

"God has a bright future and hope for my children. He designed it before I did. He will prosper my children to see their future. My children have a great future!"

PROMISES TO SPEAK THIS WEEK

1. *He gave him the plans of all that the Spirit had put in his mind.... 1 Chronicles 28:12 NIV*

2. *The plans of the Lord stand firm forever, the purposes of his heart through all generations. Psalm 33:11 NIV*

3. *The plans of the righteous are just.... Proverbs 12:5 NIV*

4. *Plans fail for lack of counsel, but with many advisers they succeed. Proverbs 15:22 NIV*

5. *Many are the plans in a person's heart, but it is the Lord's purpose that prevails. Proverbs 19:21 NIV*

6. *..."What no eye has seen, what no ear has heard, and what no human mind has conceived" — the things God has prepared for those who love him. 1 Corinthians 2:9 NIV*

7. *The purposes of a person's heart are deep waters, but one who has insight draws them out. Proverbs 20:5 NIV*

NOTES

BLESSING SIX

FULLY SUPPLIED
AND SATISFIED!

PRECEPT

I was young and now I am old, yet I have never seen the righteous forsaken or their children begging bread.

Psalm 37:25 NIV

PRINCIPLE

Your children are not beggars.

PRACTICE

Your children are not insufficient or in need. Your children do not live in mere subsistence. They are fully supplied and satisfied. They maintain a healthy appetite with choice foods. Eating disorders are caused by emotional needs and dysmorphic views of one's body. It is important that we raise our children with a healthy emotional appetite concerning food.

PROFESSION

"My children are not beggars. They are fully supplied and satisfied with food. They are healthy in their eating habits. They eat enough to be full but not too much to be gluttons. My children are not controlled by their appetites."

PROMISES TO SPEAK THIS WEEK

1. *...I said to you, "You will possess their land; I will give it to you as an inheritance, a land flowing with milk and honey." I am the Lord your God, who has set you apart from the nations. Leviticus 20:24 NIV*

2. *Eat honey, my son, for it is good; honey from the comb is sweet to your taste. Proverbs 24:13 NIV*

3. *Do not be attracted by strange, new ideas. Your strength comes from God's grace, not from rules about food, which don't help those who follow them. Hebrews 13:9 NLT*

4. *These rules may seem wise because they require strong devotion, pious self-denial, and severe bodily discipline. But they provide no help in conquering a person's evil desires. Colossians 2:23 NLT*

5. *Jesus answered, "It is written: 'Man shall not live on bread alone, but on every word that comes from the mouth of God.'" Matthew 4:4 NIV*

6. *He humbled you, causing you to hunger and then feeding you with manna, which neither you nor your ancestors had known, to teach*

you that man does not live on bread alone but on every word that comes from the mouth of the Lord. Deuteronomy 8:3 NIV

7. *When you go out to dinner with an influential person, mind your manners: Don't gobble your food, don't talk with your mouth full. And don't stuff yourself; bridle your appetite. Proverbs 23:1-3 MSG*

NOTES

_____

_____

_____

_____

_____

_____

_____

_____

_____

_____

_____

_____

_____

_____

_____

_____

_____

_____

_____

_____

_____

_____

BLESSING SEVEN

NO WEAPON OR ACCUSATION WINS!

PRECEPT

No weapon forged against you will

prevail, and you will refute every

tongue that accuses you.

Isaiah 54:17a NIV

PRINCIPLE

No unsettled claim stands against your children. No weapon forged and no forked-tongue curse can hurt your child.

PRACTICE

Unfortunately your children will face challenges and resistance from their peers as well as others. Raise your children with an assurance of God's support and defense. In Christ, there is no unsettled claim against your children. There is no accusation that can stand against them.

Bullying is at epidemic proportions in public schools. Bullies tend to prey upon the weak and vulnerable. Your children are emotionally strong and fortified against slanderous tongues. Your children will stand against them with confidence.

PROFESSION

"No weapon will win against my children. No accusation will land upon my children. My children are protected and defended by God."

PROMISES TO SPEAK THIS WEEK

1. *Do not be afraid; you will not be put to shame. Do not fear disgrace; you will not be humiliated. You will forget the shame of your youth…. Isaiah 54:4 NIV*

2. *But let no one bring a charge, let no one accuse another…. Hosea 4:4 NIV*

3. *Live such good lives among the pagans that, though they accuse you of doing wrong, they may see your good deeds and glorify God on the day he visits us. 1 Peter 2:12 NIV*

4. *The words of the reckless pierce like swords, but the tongue of the wise brings healing. Proverbs 12:18 NIV*

5. *Now he has reconciled you by Christ's physical body through death to present you holy in his sight, without blemish and free from accusation. Colossians 1:22 NIV*

6. *A thousand may fall at your side, ten thousand at your right hand, but it will not come near you. Psalm 91:7 NIV*

7. *The name of the Lord is a fortified tower; the righteous run to it and are safe. Proverbs 18:10 NIV*

NOTES

_____

_____

_____

_____

_____

_____

_____

_____

_____

_____

_____

_____

_____

_____

_____

_____

_____

_____

_____

_____

_____

_____

_____

_____

BLESSING EIGHT

GOOD NIGHTS AND SWEET DREAMS

PRECEPT

When you lie down, you will not be afraid; when you lie down, your sleep will be sweet.

Proverbs 3:24 NIV

PRINCIPLE

Children don't have to have bad dreams. Your children can be counseled in the night by the Spirit of God.

PRACTICE

Putting your children to bed can be an amazing time of bonding and instruction. By tucking your children into bed, you give them a sense of security and spiritual blessing.

Especially when my children were young, I made it a habit of tucking them into bed. I chose to tell them "faith" stories (imaginative stories that involved a child who was like them who had to use faith and wisdom to get through a circumstance). I would then pray for them with a blessing to have sweet dreams and sound sleep.

PROFESSION

"You will have sweet dreams and sound sleep. In your sleep you will have adventures without fear. The Holy Spirit will instruct you during the night. You will awaken tomorrow morning, rested and ready to face the day, in Jesus' Name. Amen."

PROMISES TO SPEAK THIS WEEK

1. *And you would be secure, because there is hope; Yes, you would dig around you, and take your rest in safety. You would also lie down, and no one would make you afraid; Yes, many would court your favor. Job 11:18-19 NKJV*

2. *I will both lie down in peace, and sleep; For You alone, O Lord, make me dwell in safety. Psalms 4:8 NKJV*

3. *Do not fear, for I have redeemed you; I have summoned you by name; you are mine. Isaiah 43:1 NIV*

4. *But whoever listens to me will live in safety and be at ease, without fear of harm. Proverbs 1:33 NIV*

5. *Because you have made the Lord, who is my refuge, Even the Most High, your dwelling place, No evil shall befall you, Nor shall any plague come near your dwelling. Psalm 91:9-10 NKJV*

6. *I lie down and sleep; I wake again, because the Lord sustains me. Psalm 3:5 NIV*

7. *My sleep had been pleasant to me. Jeremiah 31:26 NIV*

NOTES

_____

_____

_____

_____

_____

_____

_____

_____

_____

_____

_____

_____

_____

_____

_____

_____

_____

_____

_____

_____

_____

_____

BLESSING NINE

KNOWLEDGE

PRECEPT

*All your children will be
taught by the Lord, and
great will be their peace.*

Isaiah 54:13 NIV

PRINCIPLE

The Lord is interested in your children's education and intellect.

PRACTICE

That God wants your children to be educated and grow intellectually appears to be an obvious fact; however, very few fathers actively promote this truth with their children. God is concerned about children being taught. Remember, the very reason Abraham was chosen was that he would direct his children.

As a father, God is partnered with you concerning teaching your children. He is so interested in your children growing in knowledge that He promises to be personally involved. This is an amazing truth that will give you confidence in raising your children. God will support you and help you teach your children what they need to know.

I've been amazed at seeing my children grow into adulthood and surpassing what I taught them. They've learned things on their own, directly from the Lord.

How refreshing it is to know God is looking out for your children by teaching them!

PROFESSION

"My children are taught by the Lord. He instructs them. He directs their steps and orders their days. Knowing this gives my family peace. We are confident in this promise."

PROMISES TO SPEAK THIS WEEK

1. *If you are pleased with me, teach me your ways so I may know you and continue to find favor with you…. Exodus 33:13 NIV*

2. *"Teach me, and I will be quiet; show me where I have been wrong." Job 6:24 NIV*

3. *"Teach me what I cannot see; if I have done wrong, I will not do so again." Job 34:32 NIV*

4. *Show me your ways, Lord, teach me your paths. Psalm 25:4 NIV*

5. *Come, my children, listen to me; I will teach you the fear of the Lord. Psalm 34:11 NIV*

6. *Keep me from deceitful ways; be gracious to me and teach me your law. Psalm 119:29 NIV*

7. *But the Advocate, the Holy Spirit, whom the Father will send in my name, will teach you all things and will remind you of everything I have said to you. John 14:26 NIV*

NOTES

_____

_____

_____

_____

_____

_____

_____

_____

_____

_____

_____

_____

_____

_____

_____

_____

_____

_____

_____

_____

_____

_____

_____

_____

BLESSING TEN

NO FITS OF RAGE

PRECEPT

Whoever is slow to anger is better than the mighty, and he who rules his spirit than he who takes a city.

Proverbs 16:32 ESV

PRINCIPLE

The strongest child is one who can control his or her passion.

PRACTICE

We've all seen the uncontrolled temper tantrums of children. Their outbursts are embarrassing to their ill-equipped parents. Children who do not learn to control themselves are destructive and dangerous.

One purpose of discipline is to teach children to control their emotions, behavior, and passions. Failing to do so will expose them to the most volatile of all enemies — namely, themselves. One of the greatest blessings your children can learn from you is to never break out into fits of rage.

PROFESSION

"My children are not controlled by anger, rage, or violence. My children's strength is their ability to direct their passions to what is positive and good. My children rule their spirits."

PROMISES TO SPEAK THIS WEEK

1. *Refrain from anger and turn from wrath; do not fret — it leads only to evil. Psalm 37:8 NIV*

2. *Anger is cruel and fury overwhelming, but who can stand before jealousy? Proverbs 27:4 NIV*

3. *Mockers stir up a city, but the wise turn away anger. Proverbs 29:8 NIV*

4. *For as churning cream produces butter, and as twisting the nose produces blood, so stirring up anger produces strife. Proverbs 30:33 NIV*

5. *Do not be quickly provoked in your spirit, for anger resides in the lap of fools. Ecclesiastes 7:9 NIV*

6. *"In your anger do not sin:" Do not let the sun go down while you are still angry. Ephesians 4:26 NIV*

7. *Get rid of all bitterness, rage and anger, brawling and slander, along with every form of malice. Ephesians 4:31 NIV*

NOTES

PROTECTION
AND DEFENSE

PRECEPT

Whoever dwells in the shelter of the Most High will rest in the shadow of the Almighty.

Psalm 91:1 NIV

PRINCIPLE

God's love and your love are proven in the desire to protect your children.

PRACTICE

Inherent to parenting is the desire to protect your children. Although we live in a dangerous time, we have the means and ability to protect our children better than ever; however, this doesn't come without diligence.

We want to protect our children from the evils of our society. We expect our children to have safe communities, schools, and homes. We shouldn't take it for granted, but as parents we should do all we can to protect them. Protecting our children is proof of our love.

PROFESSION

"We live in the safe place of God's love. My children are shadowed by God's protection. He is always close to protect my children. No evil, harm, molestation, or violence will come upon my children. My children are safe."

PROMISES TO SPEAK THIS WEEK

1. The Lord is my strength and my defense; he has become my salvation. He is my God, and I will praise him, my father's God, and I will exalt him. Exodus 15:2 NIV

2. You, Lord, will keep the needy safe and will protect us forever from the wicked. Psalm 12:7 NIV

3. May the Lord answer you when you are in distress; may the name of the God of Jacob protect you. Psalm 20:1 NIV

4. You are my hiding place; you will protect me from trouble and surround me with songs of deliverance. Psalm 32:7 NIV

5. Do not withhold your mercy from me, Lord; may your love and faithfulness always protect me. Psalm 40:11 NIV

6. "Because he loves me," says the Lord, "I will rescue him; I will protect him, for he acknowledges my name." Psalm 91:14 NIV

7. *But the Lord is faithful, and he will strengthen you and protect you from the evil one. 2 Thessalonians 3:3 NIV*

NOTES

_____

_____

_____

_____

_____

_____

_____

_____

_____

_____

_____

_____

_____

_____

_____

_____

_____

_____

_____

_____

_____

_____

_____

_____

_____

BLESSING TWELVE

DILIGENCE

PRECEPT

Seest thou a man diligent in his business? he shall stand before kings; he shall not stand before mean men.

Proverbs 22:29 KJV

PRACTICE

We have another way of recognizing people who are diligent, we say, "He's sharp." That's exactly what the Hebrew word for diligent means. It means that a person is precise and skilled.

We want our children to be sharp. We want them to develop a skill set that will distinguish them from their peers. That skill set once developed will ensure their promotion and give them a place at the head table, so to speak.

The Message Bible says: *"Observe people who are good at their work — skilled workers are always in demand and admired; they don't take a backseat to anyone"* (Proverbs 22:29).

Your children are gifted but you will need to help develop their skills through diligence. To do so, you need to speak the blessing of diligence over your children.

PROFESSION

"My children are diligent in their skills. Others recognize their skills and admire their abilities. They are sharp. Their gifts make room for them, literally ushering them to the front of the room."

PROMISES TO SPEAK THIS WEEK

1. *Lazy hands make for poverty, but diligent hands brings wealth. Proverbs 10:4 NIV*

2. *Diligent hands will rule, but laziness ends in forced labor. Proverbs 12:24 NIV*

3. *The lazy do not roast any game, but the diligent feed on the riches of the hunt. Proverbs 12:27 NIV*

4. *The desires of the diligent are fully satisfied. Proverbs 13:4b NIV*

5. *The plans of the diligent lead to profit as surely as haste leads to poverty. Proverbs 21:5 NIV*

6. *Be diligent in these matters; give yourself wholly to them, so that everyone may see your progress. 1 Timothy 4:15 NIV*

7. Don't just do what you have to do to get by, but work heartily, as Christ's servants doing what God wants you to do. And work with a smile on your face, always keeping in mind that no matter who happens to be giving the orders, you're really serving God. Ephesians 6:6 MSG

NOTES

BLESSING THIRTEEN
FOCUSED ATTENTION

PRECEPT

Be strong and very courageous. Be careful to obey all the law my servant Moses gave you; do not turn from it to the right or to the left, that you may be successful wherever you go.

Joshua 1:7 NIV

PRINCIPLE

Men fail from a lack of focus.

PRACTICE

Attention Deficit Hyperactivity Disorder or ADHD is at epidemic proportions. Millions of children are diagnosed with ADHD, causing these children to be confined to a lifetime of drug therapy. I believe you would agree with me that this is not the will of God for your children.

Let's be faithful to speak the blessing of focus over our children.

PROFESSION

"My children are strong and courageous. They are obedient to the Word of God and are focused. My children are not double-minded. They take direction very well and they have success wherever they go."

PROMISES TO SPEAK THIS WEEK

1. *The Lord will make you the head, not the tail. If you pay attention to the commands of the Lord your God that I give you this day and carefully follow them, you will always be at the top, never at the bottom. Deuteronomy 28:13 NIV*

2. *Listen, daughter, and pay careful attention. Psalm 45:10a NIV*

3. *Listen, my sons, to a father's instruction; pay attention and gain understanding. Proverbs 4:1 NIV*

4. *We must pay the most careful attention, therefore, to what we have heard, so that we do not drift away. Hebrews 2:1 NIV*

5. *Such a person is double-minded and unstable in all they do. James 1:8 NIV*

6. *Teach me your way, Lord; lead me in a straight path because of my oppressors. Psalm 27:11 NIV*

7. *Let your eyes look straight ahead; fix your gaze directly before you. Proverbs 4:25 NIV*

NOTES

BLESSING FOURTEEN

FRIENDSHIPS

PRECEPT

Walk with the wise and become wise, for a companion of fools suffers harm.

Proverbs 13:20 NIV

PRINCIPLE

There is a residual effect of relationships. Your children's friends will influence them for good or for evil.

PRACTICE

You cannot underestimate the destructive power of simple-minded people. Your children's friends will have a profound impact on their lives. Friendships can literally become "make or break" relationships.

"Bad company corrupts good character" (1 Corinthians 15:33). Your children's friends should be good company so your children will not be enticed into evil or folly. We all know people who were collateral damage of a foolish friend. That's not going to be the case for your children. Your children will have great friends.

As our children were growing up, this was a particularly important issue for my wife. She made our children's friends a matter of daily prayer. Fortunately, my children have had good, loyal, and faithful friends. I am believing that for you.

PROFESSION

"My children have good, like-minded friends. My children's friends are loyal and trustworthy, and they are not negative influences in life. I have discernment regarding my children's friends."

PROMISES TO SPEAK THIS WEEK

1. *I am a friend to all who fear you, to all who follow your precepts. Psalm 119:63 NIV*

2. *A friend loves at all times. Proverbs 17:17a NIV*

3. *One who loves a pure heart and who speaks with grace will have the king for a friend. Proverbs 22:11 NIV*

4. *Perfume and incense bring joy to the heart, and the pleasantness of a friend springs from their heartfelt advice. Proverbs 27:9 NIV*

5. *When Jesus saw their faith, he said, "Friend, your sins are forgiven." Luke 5:20 NIV*

6. *My intercessor is my friend as my eyes pour out tears to God. Job 16:20 NIV*

7. *The righteous choose their friends carefully, but the way of the wicked leads them astray. Proverbs 12:26 NIV*

NOTES

_____

_____

_____

_____

_____

_____

_____

_____

_____

_____

_____

_____

_____

_____

_____

_____

_____

_____

_____

_____

_____

_____

_____

PATIENCE
AND ENDURANCE

PRECEPT

Patience is better

than pride.

Ecclesiastes 7:8b NIV

PRINCIPLE

Patience is a character trait of humility, as opposed to pride.

PRACTICE

We live in a microwave and fast-food era. Everything is so quick these days. It really is amazing to think about. With the advent of technology, the speed at which we can do something is incredibly fast; however, our patience has also become as quickly cooked, so to speak.

Raising children who understand the character trait of patience is not a small matter. Without patience, children will forfeit what is best for what is immediate. They will not be willing to delay gratification. Without patience, they will be prone to use credit for frivolous purchases. They won't be finishers.

Having the character trait of patience, your children will be empowered to endure to the finish, rather than being controlled by emotions or being short tempered.

PROFESSION

"My children are patient. My children have the ability to delay gratification and wait for the best to come. My children are humbled to know that the best is yet to come, and they are patiently waiting for it."

PROMISES TO SPEAK THIS WEEK

1. *May God, who gives this patience and encouragement, help you live in complete harmony with each other, as is fitting for followers of Christ Jesus. Romans 15:5 NLT*

2. *We patiently endure troubles and hardships and calamities of every kind. 2 Corinthians 6:4b NLT*

3. *You, however, know all about my teaching, my way of life, my purpose, faith, patience, love, endurance. 2 Timothy 3:10 NIV*

4. *Such things were written in the Scriptures long ago to teach us. And the Scriptures give us hope and encouragement as we wait patiently for God's promises to be fulfilled. Romans 15:4 NLT*

5. *A person's wisdom yields patience. Proverbs 19:11a NIV*

6. *We also pray that you will be strengthened with all his glorious power so you will have all the endurance and patience you need. Colossians 1:11a NLT*

7. *Then you will not become spiritually dull and indifferent. Instead, you will follow the example of those who are going to inherit God's promises because of their faith and endurance. Hebrews 6:12 NLT*

NOTES

WISDOM —THE PRINCIPAL THING!

PRECEPT

Wisdom is the principal thing; therefore get wisdom: and with all thy getting get understanding.

Proverbs 4:7 KJV

PRINCIPLE

All problems can be solved by wisdom.

PRACTICE

Wisdom is God's currency. God deals with mankind in the currency of wisdom. It really is the principal thing; frankly, it is God's tithe to us. It is the first of His creation (Proverbs 8:22). Wisdom is the governing effect of all things made by Him (Psalm 104:24). All of the laws and principles of God are wise.

Wisdom is also the ultimate success. Nothing can succeed against it. *"There is no wisdom, no insight, no plan that can succeed against the Lord"* (Proverbs 21:30 NIV). To ensure your children's success, wisdom is a blessing that you want to impart. Amazingly, God gives wisdom freely to those who ask for it (James 1:5).

Let's be sure to speak and impart wisdom to our children.

PROFESSION

"Father, you said that if anyone lacks wisdom, to ask You, and You would give wisdom generously, without finding fault. You will not be condescending to my children. My children have understanding and are wise. My children are able to comprehend the ways of God and the principles that You have put into effect. My children are problem solvers because they are wise."

PROMISES TO SPEAK THIS WEEK

1. *Wisdom, like an inheritance, is a good thing and benefits those who see the sun. Ecclesiastes 7:11 NIV*

2. *A man who loves wisdom brings joy to his father. Proverbs 29:3a NIV*

3. *Wisdom makes one wise person more powerful than ten rulers in a city. Ecclesiastes 7:19 NIV*

4. *Know also that wisdom is like honey for you: If you find it, there is a future hope for you, and your hope will not be cut off. Proverbs 24:14 NIV*

5. *Wisdom is a shelter as money is a shelter, but the advantage of knowledge is this: Wisdom preserves those who have it. Ecclesiastes 7:12 NIV*

6. *"I have heard of you, that the Spirit of God is in you, and that light and understanding and excellent wisdom are found in you." Daniel 5:14 NKJV*

7. *...Wisdom is proved right by all her children. Luke 7:35 NIV*

NOTES

_____

_____

_____

_____

_____

_____

_____

_____

_____

_____

_____

_____

_____

_____

_____

_____

_____

_____

_____

_____

_____

BLESSING SEVENTEEN

REWARDING WORK

PRECEPT

*But as for you, be strong
and do not give up,
for your work will
be rewarded.*

2 Chronicles 15:7 NIV

PRINCIPLE

Labor is subsistence living; while work is designed to be rewarding.

PRACTICE

Most people are very confused concerning work and labor. God created us with directional intent and purpose. God worked. He created man to work, so we have *a vocation*, which means *a divinely-spoken-calling.* Before the fall, Adam simply planted seed and reaped an unfettered harvest. Only after the fall of mankind did work become associated with labor.

Labor does not come with the enjoyment and fulfillment of achievement. It's hard, and it's a drudgery. Everything that you do is resisted. Adam experienced thorns and weeds when he labored.

Labor is subsistence living. It simply is maintenance and brings no reward to you. Most people live a life of maintenance — just getting by week to week. Obviously, we want more for our children than simply making it. We don't want them laboring through life; we want them fulfilling their vocation — God's spoken call upon them.

It's important to raise our children to understand that work is a blessing and they will be rewarded in it.

PROFESSION

"My children are created on purpose and for a purpose. My children are blessed in their work. My children do not labor in vain and aren't just getting by; but they are fulfilling their vocation, God's calling upon them. My children are strong and resilient to get the job done and do it well."

PROMISES TO SPEAK THIS WEEK

1. *Laban said to him, "Just because you are a relative of mine, should you work for me for nothing? Tell me what your wages should be." Genesis 29:15 NIV*

2. *Then Moses summoned Bezalel and Oholiab and every skilled person to whom the Lord had given ability and who was willing to come and do the work. Exodus 36:2 NIV*

3. *They were just trying to intimidate us, imagining that they could discourage us and stop the work. So I continued the work with even greater determination. Nehemiah 6:9 NLT*

4. *They realized this work had been done with the help of our God. Nehemiah 6:16b NLT*

5. *It is useless for you to work so hard from early morning until late at night, anxiously working for food to eat; for God gives rest to his loved ones. Psalm 127:2 NLT*

6. *Work hard and become a leader; be lazy and become a slave. Proverbs 12:24 NLT*

7. *All hard work brings a profit, but mere talk leads only to poverty. Proverbs 14:23 NIV*

NOTES

_____

_____

_____

_____

_____

_____

_____

_____

_____

_____

_____

_____

_____

_____

_____

_____

JOYFUL COUNTENANCE

PRECEPT

*How joyful are those who
fear the Lord and delight
in obeying his commands.*

Psalm 112:1b NLT

PRINCIPLE

Joy is strength.

PRACTICE

Joy brightens a person's countenance. It's hard to hide joy. Joy is expressive. When a person is joyful, it often manifests with a physical expression, such as, jumping, running, or dancing. It also is usually loud, shouting, singing, etc.

Joy is different than happiness. Happiness is usually confined to the circumstances of the moment, while joy is an expression of complete satisfaction. There is a remarkable difference when you see a happy child and a joyful child. A happy child is usually only that way because of the temporary circumstances of the moment; a joyful child seems complete.

Another trademark of a joyful child is that joyfulness gives them strength. To be joyful is to be resilient. I know you want your children to have a joyful countenance.

PROFESSION

"Lord, let my children be joyful and glad. Let them jump with excitement about life. May all those who know them see the expression of joy in their lives, the complete satisfaction of serving You and knowing Your goodness. Let their happiness not be temporarily tied to the circumstances of life. My children are joyful!"

PROMISES TO SPEAK THIS WEEK

1. *The Lord is my strength and my shield; my heart trusts in him, and he helps me. My heart leaps for joy, and with my song I praise him. Psalm 28:7 NIV*

2. *You have turned my mourning into joyful dancing. You have taken away my clothes of mourning and clothed me with joy. Psalm 30:11 NLT*

3. *Yes, the Lord has done amazing things for us! What joy! Psalm 126:3 NLT*

4. *A wise son brings joy to his father. Proverbs 15:20a NIV*

5. *Evil people are trapped by sin, but the righteous escape, shouting for joy. Proverbs 29:6 NLT*

6. *And the believers were filled with joy and with the Holy Spirit. Acts 13:52 NLT*

7. *In all my prayers for all of you, I always pray with joy. Philippians 1:4 NIV*

NOTES

_____

_____

_____

_____

_____

_____

_____

_____

_____

_____

_____

_____

_____

_____

_____

_____

_____

_____

_____

_____

BLESSING NINETEEN

ORDERED STEPS

★ ★ ★ ★ ★

PRECEPT

My steps have held to your paths; my feet have not stumbled.

Psalm 17:5 NIV

PRINCIPLE

God leads us in steps, not in leaps.

PRACTICE

One of the greatest misconceptions about the Lord's leading is that He demands that we take a "leap of faith." I would contend that the only one in the Bible to suggest taking a leap of faith was satan, when he tempted Jesus saying, "If you are the Son of God, jump!" (Matthew 4:6)

It has become Christian folklore that we are asked to take a leap of faith — that whenever we come to a cliff, we should jump and "trust God." I would argue that suggesting to our children to jump off a cliff is presumptive.

How does God lead us? He orders our steps. As I stated before, God relates to men in the daily commute.

Steps are easy. Leaps are difficult. Steps are doable. Leaps are dangerous. I recommend teaching your children how to take steps.

PROFESSION

"My children's steps are ordered. They are directed by the Lord. Righteousness goes before them and prepares their way. My children are not hampered. They will not stumble. They do not turn to one side or the other, but they go straight toward their destiny."

PROMISES TO SPEAK THIS WEEK

1. *For then you would guard my steps, instead of watching for my sins. Job 14:16 NLT*

2. *My feet have closely followed his steps; I have kept to his way without turning aside. Job 23:11 NIV*

3. *The Lord directs the steps of the godly. He delights in every detail of their lives. Psalm 37:23 NLT*

4. *Righteousness goes before him and prepares the way for his steps. Psalm 85:13 NIV*

5. *When you walk, your steps will not be hampered; when you run, you will not stumble. Proverbs 4:12 NIV*

6. *A person's steps are directed by the Lord. Proverbs 20:24 NIV*

7. *To this you were called, because Christ suffered for you, leaving you an example, that you should follow in his steps. 1 Peter 2:21 NIV*

NOTES

_____

_____

_____

_____

_____

_____

_____

_____

_____

_____

_____

_____

_____

_____

_____

_____

_____

_____

_____

_____

_____

_____

_____

NO STRIFE IN MY CHILD'S LIFE!

PRECEPT

For where you have envy and selfish ambition, there you find disorder and every evil practice.

James 3:16 NIV

PRINCIPLE

Where there is strife, there is every form of evil.

PRACTICE

The atmosphere of your home is a huge player in the raising of emotionally healthy children. Seriously, strife is dangerous. Don't play with it.

Studies suggest that more than ten million children witness some form of domestic violence annually. A strife-filled home is a horrible place to live. Strife is the manifested presence of satan. Protect your home. Don't allow strife to take residence there. Make your home a safe place, a strife-free zone.

Honestly, this is one of my biggest wins in life, keeping strife out of my home. My wife and I never argued in front of our children. Even our private disagreements were carefully communicated. I know that sounds impossible, but it's not if you protect your home from strife.

One of the quickest ways to keep strife out of your home is to keep yourself from being entertained by it on television. People often allow arguments to come into their living rooms through TV. You can feel strife in the room. It is a real force to be dealt with, so set the tone of your home by keeping strife out.

PROFESSION

"Our home is a refuge. It is free from strife. It is filled with love. My children feel safe here. We have a hedge of protection around our home. We do not allow the enemy to gain access into our home; not through television, the Internet, phones, family, or friends. Our home is a fortress of faith."

PROMISES TO SPEAK THIS WEEK

1. *In peace I will lie down and sleep, for you alone, Lord, make me dwell in safety. Psalm 4:8 NIV*

2. *Turn from evil and do good; seek peace and pursue it. Psalm 34:14 NIV*

3. Love and faithfulness meet together; righteousness and peace kiss each other. Psalm 85:10 NIV

4. May there be peace within your walls and security within your citadels. Psalm 122:7 NIV

5. Deceit is in the hearts of those who plot evil, but those who promote peace have joy. Proverbs 12:20 NIV

6. Better a dry crust with peace and quiet than a house full of feasting with strife. Proverbs 17:1 NIV

7. If the home is deserving, let your peace rest on it; if it is not, let your peace return to you. Matthew 10:13 NIV

NOTES

_____

_____

_____

_____

_____

_____

_____

_____

_____

_____

_____

_____

_____

_____

_____

_____

_____

_____

CHAPTER TWENTY-ONE
ASSIGNMENT

PRECEPT

Before I formed you in the womb I knew [and] approved of you [as My chosen instrument], and before you were born I separated and set you apart, consecrating you; [and] I appointed you as a prophet to the nations.

Jeremiah 1:5 AMP

PRINCIPLE

You can't dream a dream greater than the dream God has for your children.

PRACTICE

The depth of love you have for your child seems immeasurable. It would be difficult to think that someone could dream a bigger dream for your child than you can. God can. God does. God has a bigger and better dream for your child than you do. How is that possible?

Because God knew your child before you did. He fashioned your child in the sacred womb of a mother. He specifically designed the person that he or she is to become. Then God did something even more amazing. He crafted holy plans, assignments, appointments, and purposes for your child.

That's why it's important for us to be speaking blessing over our children. We want God's assignment to be fulfilled, which requires our cooperation and will to make the appointments. Fathering is more than protection and provision; it's helping shape the vision that God has for your children.

PROFESSION

"Father, You designed and shaped my children in the womb of their mother. You have holy plans for them. Their purpose was conceived in You before they became living beings. Give us the ability to know what You've dreamed for them. Give my children insight into their appointments, in Jesus' Name. Amen."

PROMISES TO SPEAK THIS WEEK

1. *You discern my going out and my lying down; you are familiar with all my ways. Psalm 139:3 NIV*

2. *For you created my inmost being; you knit me together in my mother's womb. Psalm 139:13 NIV*

3. *I praise you because I am fearfully and wonderfully made; your works are wonderful, I know that full well. Psalm 139:14 NIV*

4. *How precious to me are your thoughts, God! How vast is the sum of them! Psalm 139:17 NIV*

5. *"…Who knows but that you have come to your royal position for such a time as this?" Esther 4:14b NIV*

6. *I can do all this through him who gives me strength. Philippians 4:13 NIV*

7. *Therefore, since we are surrounded by such a great cloud of witnesses, let us throw off everything that hinders and the sin that so easily entangles. And let us run with perseverance the race marked out for us. Hebrews 12:1 NIV*

NOTES

_____

_____

_____

_____

_____

_____

_____

_____

_____

_____

_____

_____

_____

_____

_____

_____

_____

_____

_____

_____

BLESSING TWENTY-TWO
CHURCH

PRECEPT

One thing I ask from the Lord, this only do I seek: that I may dwell in the house of the Lord all the days of my life, to gaze on the beauty of the Lord and to seek him in his temple.

Psalm 27:4-5 NIV

PRINCIPLE

Where you are determines what grows within you.

PRACTICE

Your children need a great church to connect with — not only for what they will get out of it, but for what they can give to it. Selecting a viable church is a very important decision that shouldn't be made out of tradition or convenience. As fathers, we need to look for biblical patterns of behavior and teaching that comes from the leadership. Do the leaders manage their own households well? Do the leaders' families model Christian faith and bear fruit?

The Church has changed and adapted its methodology to relate to culture; however, the essentials of the Church have remained timeless. In Acts 2:42-47, eight essentials in church functions are revealed: sound doctrine, fellowship, communion, prayer, spiritual gifts, equality, giving, and worship.

PROFESSION

"Father, we pray for the Church. Give us wisdom and direction to find the congregation where my children will be protected and spiritually nourished. We pray for a local church that reflects Your character and will be empowered by Your Spirit. We pray for the leadership of the church to lead with character and conviction according to the Word of God."

PROMISES TO SPEAK THIS WEEK

1. *And I tell you that you are Peter, and on this rock I will build my church, and the gates of Hades will not overcome it. Matthew 16:18 NIV*

2. *Then the church throughout Judea, Galilee and Samaria enjoyed a time of peace and was strengthened. Living in the fear of the Lord and encouraged by the Holy Spirit, it increased in numbers. Acts 9:31 NIV*

3. *...Since you are eager for gifts of the Spirit, try to excel in those that build up the church. 1 Corinthians 14:12 NIV*

4. God placed all things under his feet and appointed him to be head over everything for the church. Ephesians 1:22 NIV

5. His intent was that now, through the church, the manifold wisdom of God should be made known to the rulers and authorities in the heavenly realms. Ephesians 3:10 NIV

6. Now as the church submits to Christ, so also wives should submit to their husbands in everything. Ephesians 5:24 NIV

7. If anyone does not know how to manage his own family, how can he take care of God's church? 1 Timothy 3:5 NIV

NOTES

_____

_____

_____

_____

_____

_____

_____

_____

_____

_____

_____

_____

_____

_____

_____

_____

_____

_____

BLESSING TWENTY-THREE

ACCOUNTABILITY

PRECEPT

Now all has been heard; here is the conclusion of the matter: Fear God and keep his commandments, for this is the duty of all mankind. For God will bring every deed into judgment, including every hidden thing, whether it is good or evil.

Ecclesiastes 12:13-14 NIV

PRINCIPLE

Children do what you inspect, not what you expect.

PRACTICE

When you give your children an instruction, it's important to hold them accountable. Holding your children accountable will prove to be a tremendous blessing in their lives. It will help them succeed at the highest level.

U.S. Navy Admiral William H. McCraven, Commander of the U.S. Special Operations Command, the commander who oversaw the raid to kill Osama Bin Laden, during his commencement speech at the University of Texas, gave this key to success for children, "If you make your bed every morning, you will have accomplished the first task of the day. It will give you a small sense of pride, and it will encourage you to do another task, and another, and another. And by the end of the day that one task completed will have turned into many tasks completed."

Commander McCraven also said, "Be your very best in the darkest moment."

I call this "The Closet Principle" — what you do in secret is what moves you in public.

PROFESSION

"Father, I know that holding my children accountable is an important blessing in their lives. Help me be aware of the good things they do and acknowledge them. Also, Lord, help me not to brush aside the things that they have done wrong. Give me the courage to hold them accountable to do things right so they know what is expected of them, in Jesus' Name. Amen."

PROMISES TO SPEAK THIS WEEK

1. *Lord, what is man that thou takest knowledge of him! or the son of man, that thou makest account of him! Psalm 144:3 KJV*

2. He would surely call you to account if you secretly showed partiality. *Job 13:10 NIV*

3. I would give him an account of my every step; I would present it to him as to a ruler. *Job 31:37 NIV*

4. I gave an account of my ways and you answered me; teach me your decrees. *Psalm 119:26 NIV*

5. So then, each of us will give an account of ourselves to God. *Romans 14:12 NIV*

6. Have confidence in your leaders and submit to their authority, because they keep watch over you as those who must give an account. Do this so that their work will be a joy, not a burden, for that would be of no benefit to you. *Hebrews 13:17 NIV*

7. They will have to give account to him who is ready to judge the living and the dead. *1 Peter 4:5 NIV*

NOTES

BLESSING TWENTY-FOUR

TITHING

★ ★ ★ ★ ★

PRECEPT

And without doubt

the lesser is blessed

by the greater.

Hebrews 7:7 NIV

PRINCIPLE

Tithing positions a person under the blessing of Christ, as High Priest.

PRACTICE

Tithing is giving the first ten percent of your increase or wages to the Lord. Teaching your children the principle of tithing will guarantee them a life of blessing. Those who argue against the practice of tithing do so out of ignorance of Scripture and at their own demise.

Abel, the second son of Adam, was the first person to give the tithe; he gave the best portion of the firstborn of his flock as an offering to the Lord. As a result, God showed favor to Abel and his offering.

Years later, Abraham gave the first tenth to the High Priest, Melchizedek, who served as the Prince of Salem (Peace). Moses instituted the practice of tithing in the Law as foundational for those who live under the covenant. One of the offices that Jesus holds is in the order of Melchizedek, which predates the Levitical law of tithing, and our tithe is given in that order. Therefore, tithing is not an Old Testament law without practice in the New Testament.

If you want to ensure that your children are blessed financially to meet their needs, to fulfill their desires in life, and to finance their purpose, teach them to tithe.

PROFESSION

"I will show honor to God by teaching my children to tithe. I will demonstrate my victory over greed and materialism by giving and worshipping God first with all of my income. Jesus speaks the blessing over our tithe as a family and all we do will prosper so we have all of our needs met, God will grant the desires of our hearts, and we can finance our purpose in life."

PROMISES TO SPEAK THIS WEEK

1. *A tithe of everything from the land, whether grain from the soil or fruit from the trees, belongs to the Lord; it is holy to the Lord. Leviticus 27:30 NIV*

2.   Then Melchizedek king of Salem brought out bread and wine. He was priest of God Most High, and he blessed Abram, saying, "Blessed be Abram by God Most High, Creator of heaven and earth. And praise be to God Most High, who delivered your enemies into your hand." Then Abram gave him a tenth of everything. Genesis 14:18-21 NIV

3.   "Bring the whole tithe into the storehouse, that there my be food in my house. Test me in this," says the Lord Almighty, "and see if I will not throw open the floodgates of heaven and pour out so much blessing that there will not be room enough to store it." Malachi 3:10 NIV

4.   Then Jacob made a vow, saying, "If God will be with me and will watch over me on this journey I am taking and will give me food to eat and clothes to wear so that I return safely to my father's household, then the Lord will be my God and this stone that I have set up as a pillar will be God's house, and of all that you give me I will give you a tenth." Genesis 28:20-22 NIV

5.   Honor the Lord with your wealth, with the first fruits of all your crops; then your barns will be filled to overflowing, and your vats will brim over with new wine. Proverbs 3:9-10 NIV

6.   ...Whoever sows sparingly will also reap sparingly; whoever sows generously will also reap generously. Each of you should give what you have decided in your heart to give, not reluctantly or under compulsion, for God loves a cheerful giver. And God is able to bless you abundantly, so that in all things at all times, having all that you need, you will abound in every good work. 2 Corinthians 9:6-8 NIV

7.   This man, however, did not trace his descent from Levi, yet he collected a tenth from Abraham and blessed him who had the promises. And without doubt the lesser is blessed by the greater. Hebrews 7:6-7 NIV

NOTES

BLESSING TWENTY-FIVE

FAVOR!

PRECEPT

Glory to God in the highest heaven, and on earth peace to those on whom his favor rests.

Luke 2:14 NIV

PRINCIPLE

Favor is a gift from God — a supernatural force to work on your behalf to accomplish your purpose.

PRACTICE

Favor works much like a current that moves you and works on your behalf. There is something very special when a father sees the favor of God work on behalf of his children. It is humbling. It is awe inspiring.

"Jesus grew in favor with God and man" (Luke 2:52). Your child can grow in favor with God and with men. There should be a day that you exclaim, "This is my son, in whom I am well pleased." This kind of affirmation is a tremendous force for your children.

Abel received favor after he tithed. Noah received favor in a wicked generation. Abraham received favor to receive the promise of his son Isaac. Moses received favor as an infant and was protected because his mother realized he was special. The entire story of Esther reveals how an orphan girl became a queen because favor positioned her and promoted her above her peers, elevating her into the palace.

PROFESSION

"My children have God's favor. May favor open doors for them. May favor give them the best place for their purpose. God will give them favor with those in authority — teachers, coaches, administrators, etc. Let favor escort my children into the place of honor. I give them my favor. I am well pleased with them. God will show them His favor and grant them the assurance of His confidence."

PROMISES TO SPEAK THIS WEEK

1. *Abel also brought an offering — fat portions from some of the firstborn of his flock. The Lord looked with favor on Abel and his offering. Genesis 4:4 NIV*

2. *But Noah found favor in the eyes of the Lord. Genesis 6:8 NIV*

3. *Abraham said, "If I have found favor in your eyes, my lord, do not pass your servant by." Genesis 18:3 NIV*

4. Remember me with favor, my God, for all I have done for these people. Nehemiah 5:19 NIV

5. She pleased him and won his favor.... Esther 2:9a NIV

6. Surely, Lord, you bless the righteous; you surround them with your favor as with a shield. Psalm 5:12 NIV

7. You will lie down, with no one to make you afraid, and many will court your favor. Job 11:19 NIV

NOTES

BLESSING TWENTY-SIX

TEMPTATION

★ ★ ★ ★ ★

PRECEPT

Lead us not into temptation, but deliver us from the evil one.

Matthew 6:13 NIV

PRINCIPLE

Temptation is an enticement to sin, arising from inward desires or outward circumstances.

PRACTICE

We want our children to avoid the entrapments of sin. We want them to avoid the dangerous pitfalls of life, such as, drugs, alcohol, and sexual sin. Too many children are destroyed by such things.

Let's raise up children who have the ability to walk away from something that they desire in order to protect something else that they love. Train your children to deny present appetites for future rewards. This is very countercultural, but it will empower your children. It will help them be in the driver's seat when it comes to making decisions.

Overcoming temptation will protect your children from the common pitfalls of peer pressure. They will have a higher standard for themselves and protect their personal dignity with a self-assurance that comes from their identity in Christ.

PROFESSION

"Father, please protect my children from the temptations of evil. Give them mastery over their decisions. Let them know who they are in Christ Jesus and identify with Him. Let their peers see their high standard of living and refrain from enticing them to do evil, in Jesus' Name. Amen."

PROMISES TO SPEAK THIS WEEK

1. *Do not harden your hearts, as in the rebellion, as in the day of trial in the wilderness. Psalm 95:8 NKJV*

2. *Watch and pray so that you may not enter into temptation. The spirit indeed is willing, but the flesh is weak. Matthew 26:41 ESV*

3. *When the devil had finished all this tempting, he left him until an opportune time. Luke 4:13 NIV*

4. *No temptation has overtaken you that is not common to man. God is faithful, and he will not let you be tempted beyond your ability,*

but with the temptation he will also provide the way of escape, that you may be able to endure it. 1 Corinthians 10:13 NKJV

5. *But those who desire to be rich fall into temptation and a snare, and into many foolish and harmful lusts which drown men in destruction and perdition. 1 Timothy 6:9 NKJV*

6. *Blessed is the man who endures temptation; for when he has been approved, he will receive the crown of life which the Lord has promised to those who love Him. James 1:12 NIV*

7. *Because thou hast kept the word of my patience, I also will keep thee from the hour of temptation, which shall come upon all the world, to try them that dwell upon the earth. Revelation 3:10 KJV*

NOTES

_____

_____

_____

_____

_____

_____

_____

_____

_____

_____

_____

_____

_____

_____

_____

_____

_____

_____

BLESSING TWENTY-SEVEN
INTEGRITY

PRECEPT

For the upright will inhabit the land, and those with integrity will remain in it.

Proverbs 2:21 ESV

PRINCIPLE

Integrity is the standard of measure for correctness. It is straightening out what is crooked.

PRACTICE

Having integrity will guard your children from perverted tracks, paths that are dangerous and morally deficient. When considering a decision, integrity will give your children the ability to align that decision with what is straight. It helps them forecast the outcome of their path.

Integrity makes your children ready-minded and prompt in decisions; they won't have a tendency to waffle in indecision. A double-minded person is unstable in all their decisions; they lack integrity.

Integrity also gives your children stability of the moment and a hope for their future. They have nothing to fear, nothing hidden to be discovered. Integrity is also a part of "The Closet Principle" — what you do in secret is what moves you in public. Integrity makes your children secure in their own home.

PROFESSION

"My children's hearts lead them with integrity. They have ready-minds and are quick to decide by the standard of what is right. My children are established in integrity. They know the way of truth and are guided by their hope for the future."

PROMISES TO SPEAK THIS WEEK

1. *In the integrity of my heart and the innocence of my hands I have done this. Genesis 20:5 ESV*

2. *And as for you, if you will walk before me, as David your father walked, with integrity of heart and uprightness, doing according to all that I have commanded you, and keeping my statues and my rules, then I will establish your royal throne over Israel forever.... 1 Kings 9:4-5 ESV*

3. *Is not your fear of God your confidence, and the integrity of your ways your hope? Job 4:6 ESV*

4. *The Lord judges the peoples; judge me, O Lord, according to my righteousness and according to the integrity that is in me. Psalm 7:8 ESV*

5. *I will ponder the way that is blameless. Oh when will you come to me? I will walk with integrity of heart within my house. Psalm 101:2 ESV*

6. *Whoever walks in integrity walks securely, but he who makes his ways crooked will be found out. Proverbs 10:9 ESV*

7. *The righteous who walks in his integrity — blessed are his children after him. Proverbs 20:7 ESV*

NOTES

_____

_____

_____

_____

_____

_____

_____

_____

_____

_____

_____

_____

_____

_____

_____

_____

BLESSING TWENTY-EIGHT
COMPASSION

PRECEPT

And of some have compassion, making a difference.

Jude 1:22 KJV

PRINCIPLE

Compassion refers to disturbing the emotions of a person's heart, an unsettling that moves a person to action.

PRACTICE

We've grown accustomed to seeing very disturbing commercials of starving children. The emotions that move us during those commercials, those motivational urges to move into action — that's compassion. When we're moved with compassion we are motivated to do something.

Raising children who have a heart for social justice is a goal that we should have. Children who can recognize the suffering and feel the pain of others are good, but even more than simply feeling their pain, we want them to be moved to relieve it. If our children don't have a cause worth fighting for they'll find the wrong thing to fight against.

When Moses saw the injustice of an Egyptian slave being beaten, he was moved with compassion to bring justice. His compassion positioned him as a leader who would lead his people out of bondage.

Compassion is a powerful attribute that God shows toward us and a value that we should establish in our children.

PROFESSION

"Father, help me show compassion for those who are in need, for those who are less fortunate in life. I want to model for my children how to take action to deliver people from injustice. Give my children eyes that are open to see hurting people. Give them hearts that are full of mercy. Give them strong hands to lift their burdens. Give them the means to finance their purpose in life, in Jesus' Name. Amen."

PROMISES TO SPEAK THIS WEEK

1. For the Lord will vindicate his people and have compassion on his servants, when he sees that their power is gone and there is none remaining, bond or free. Deuteronomy 32:36 ESV

2. And Saul said, "May you be blessed by the Lord, for you have had compassion on me." 1 Samuel 23:21 ESV

3. For the Lord will give justice to his people and have compassion on his servants. Psalm 135:14 NLT

4. For a brief moment I deserted you, but with great compassion I will gather you. Isaiah 54:7 ESV

5. When he saw the crowds, he had compassion for them, because they were harassed and helpless, like sheep without a shepherd. Matthew 9:36 ESV

6. When he went ashore he saw a great crowd, and he had compassion on them and healed their sick. Matthew 14:14 ESV

7. For he says to Moses, "I will have mercy on whom I have mercy, and I will have compassion on whom I have compassion." Romans 9:15 ESV

NOTES

BLESSING TWENTY-NINE
OBEDIENCE

★ ★ ★ ★ ★

PRECEPT

Children, obey your parents in everything, for this pleases the Lord.

Colossians 3:20 ESV

PRINCIPLE

God places you under authority so that you can master what He has placed you over.

PRACTICE

The Greek word for **obedient** means **under a voice.** As the parent, you give directional intent for your children. As they listen to your voice, you guide them and give them direction.

One Easter, when my children were young, I hid eggs for them to find. My two oldest, Alexandra and Chase, had an advantage over my third child, Courtney. To help Courtney I whispered in her ear, "Courtney, go toward that big tree." She took off running to the tree. When she got there I motioned for her to go around it and look down. She followed my lead and found a prized egg.

That's what the Word of God does for us. When we read it, we hear the whispering words of the Holy Spirit, "Go in that direction and you will find something I've hidden for you." The lesson here is that God often hides something **for** us; He is not hiding something **from** us.

Obedience actually gives us ears to hear. The instructions we obey determine the rewards that we gain.

PROFESSION

"My children are obedient in life. They hear God's voice, but the voice of a stranger they will not follow. A strange voice will not captivate them. I am placed under God's leadership so that I can lead my children. God gives me wisdom to do so."

PROMISES TO SPEAK THIS WEEK

1. *Walk in obedience to all that the Lord your God has commanded you, so that you may live and prosper and prolong your days in the land that you will possess. Deuteronomy 5:33 NIV*

2. *Observe the commands of the Lord your God, walking in obedience to him and revering him. Deuteronomy 8:6 NIV*

3. *But be very careful to keep the commandment and law that Moses the servant of the Lord gave you: to love the Lord your God, to walk in obedience to him, to keep his commands, to hold fast to him and to serve him with all your heart and with your soul. Joshua 22:5 NIV*

4. *If you walk in obedience to me and keep my decrees and commands as David your father did, I will give you a long life. 1 Kings 3:14 NIV*

5. *Blessed are all who fear the Lord, who walk in obedience to him. Psalm 128:1 NIV*

6. *For just as through the disobedience of the one man the many were made sinners, so also through the obedience of the one man the many will be made righteous. Romans 5:19 NIV*

7. *And this is love: that we walk in obedience to his commands. As you have heard from the beginning, his command is that you walk in love. 2 John 1:6 NIV*

NOTES

_____

_____

_____

_____

_____

_____

_____

_____

_____

_____

_____

_____

_____

_____

_____

BLESSING THIRTY
CONFIDENCE

★ ★ ★ ★ ★

PRECEPT

Blessed is the one who trusts in the Lord, whose confidence is in him.

Jeremiah 17:7 NIV

PRINCIPLE

Confidence is putting one's hope, trust, and personal security in the Lord.

PRACTICE

My family and I recently had dinner with a businessman. The conversation became very interesting as he began to ask my children questions. He asked, "What did your father do so that you were raised to have such confidence to speak with adults and carry yourselves with respect?"

All three of my young adult children responded in a similar way, "Our parents always treated us with respect and expected to be treated with respect."

One of the greatest lessons I have learned is to treat my children as brothers and sisters in the Lord and not just as my children. This caused me not to treat them as common. I treated them with mutual respect. The byproduct of this principle allowed my children to have a confidence in the Lord. It gave them a direct pathway to God, as Father. They relate to Him personally. Their confidence is in Him.

PROFESSION

"Father, my children are Your children. You knew them before I knew them. You are their Heavenly Father, and they have confidence in You. I know that You will lead them. I know that You will protect them. Their hope is in You. Give me the ability to treat them with mutual respect, as they are truly my brothers and sisters in Christ, in Jesus' Name. Amen."

PROMISES TO SPEAK THIS WEEK

1. *Such confidence we have through Christ before God. 2 Corinthians 3:4 NIV*

2. *I am glad I can have complete confidence in you. 2 Corinthians 7:16 NIV*

3. *In him and through faith in him we may approach God with freedom and confidence. Ephesians 3:12 NIV*

4. *So do not throw away your confidence; it will be richly rewarded. Hebrews 10:35 NIV*

5. *Now faith is confidence in what we hope for and assurance about what we do not see. Hebrews 11:1 NIV*

6. *So we say with confidence, "The Lord is my helper; I will not be afraid. What can mere mortals do to me?" Hebrews 13:6 NIV*

7. *This is the confidence we have in approaching God: that if we ask anything according to his will, he hears us. 1 John 5:14 NIV*

NOTES

_____

_____

_____

_____

_____

_____

_____

_____

_____

_____

_____

_____

_____

_____

_____

_____

_____

_____

_____

_____

_____

BLESSING THIRTY-ONE

DREAMS

PRECEPT

For God does speak — now one way, now another — though no one perceives it. In a dream, in a vision of the night, when deep sleep falls on people as they slumber in their beds, He may speak in their ears and terrify them with warnings, to turn them from wrongdoing and keep them from pride.

Job 33:14-17 NIV

PRINCIPLE

Don't waste another night just sleeping. Allow the counsel of the Holy Spirit to instruct you.

PRACTICE

Historically, most civilizations regarded dreams as important to our emotional state, helpful in problem solving, and prophetically giving us warnings about threatening events.

Biblically, there is no doubt that God uses dreams to communicate things to us. There may be many reasons for God choosing to use the language of dreams. We are often so distracted by immediate needs and concerns that we rarely forecast our future with careful thought and planning. Another reason dreams are often used of God is that He knows the future and we don't. He is able to give us promptings and warnings concerning things to come.

There is no doubt that most of those who have been used of God for special assignments and callings received dreams. Those dreams were helpful to shape their lives and gave them confidence to pursue the future.

Joseph is a great example of a young man who received a dream. That dream became so powerful in his life that others actually envied him for having the dream. Imagine how paranoid his brothers had to be to fear the internal vision of Joseph's dream so much that they were willing to commit murder to stop it.

We want to raise our children with the ability to dream dreams. We want God to give them a divinely illustrated portrait to pursue.

PROFESSION

"Father, speak to my children tonight in their dreams. I pray that the Holy Spirit will counsel them about their lives. Whatever is important to them tomorrow, I pray You will give them insight concerning it tonight. I also ask that You will give me discernment to help and not hinder the dreams that You give them, in Jesus' Name. Amen."

PROMISES TO SPEAK THIS WEEK

1. *A dream comes when there are many cares…. Ecclesiastes 5:3a NIV*

2. *Then God said to him in the dream, "Yes, I know you did this with a clear conscience, and so I have kept you from sinning against me…." Genesis 20:6 NIV*

3. *He had a dream in which he saw a stairway resting on the earth, with its top reaching to heaven, and the angels of God were ascending and descending on it. Genesis 28:12 NIV*

4. *"The angel of God said to me in the dream. 'Jacob.'" I answered, "Here I am." Genesis 31:11 NIV*

5. *He said to them, "Listen to this dream I had…." Genesis 37:6 NIV*

6. *I will pour out my Spirit on all people. Your sons and daughters will prophesy, your old men will dream dreams, your young men will see visions. Joel 2:28 NIV*

7. *And having been warned in a dream not to go back to Herod, they returned to their country by another route. Matthew 2:12 NIV*

NOTES

_____

_____

_____

_____

_____

_____

_____

_____

_____

_____

_____

_____

_____

BLESSING THIRTY-TWO
THE BREAD OF LIFE

PRECEPT

Jesus answered, "It is written: 'Man shall not live on bread alone, but on every word that comes from the mouth of God.'"

Matthew 4:4 NIV

PRINCIPLE

Just as we provide our children with a healthy diet, we also provide them with their spiritual food.

PRACTICE

Through the Word of God all things were made; without the Word of God nothing was made that has been made (John 1:3). It is also revealed that in the Word of God is life. That being said, if the Word of God was necessary to create life, it is also necessary to sustain life.

That places a supreme importance on a daily discipline of reading and hearing the Word of God. Abstaining from the Word of God spiritually would be equivalent to starving ourselves physically. We would be diagnosed with an eating disorder and become unhealthy, malnourished and sickly. We wouldn't do that to our children physically. We certainly shouldn't do that to our children spiritually.

Some men have failed to provide the Word of God for their children. They leave it to their wives or delegate it to the Church. However, men are responsible for providing for their families. Fathers are responsible to teach their children the Word.

Don't be uncomfortable teaching the Word to your children. You may say, "I don't know enough about the Word of God to teach it." Don't excuse yourself that way. Take a few minutes each day and read the Bible. You'll be surprised to find that the Holy Spirit will give you specific insight on what your children need to nourish them. I recommend that you start with Proverbs, which is loaded with teachable principles. Don't try to overdo it; just do a little at a time. Don't be complicated. Make it simple enough to learn.

PROFESSION

"I am a good teacher of the Word to my children. God knows what they need more than I do, so I yield to His Spirit to help me. As I read the Word of God, I receive insight and understanding on how it pertains to life. I want to know God's ways and do them. I accept the responsibility to train up my children in the way they should go."

PROMISES TO SPEAK THIS WEEK

1. *Every Word of God is flawless; he is a shield to those who take refuge in him. Proverbs 30:5 NIV*

2. *This is the meaning of the parable: The seed is the word of God. Luke 8:11 NIV*

3. *Take the helmet of salvation and the sword of the Spirit, which is the word of God. Ephesians 6:17 NIV*

4. *…God gave me to present to you the Word of God in its fullness. Colossians 1:25 NIV*

5. *…Blessed rather are those who hear the Word of God and obey it. Luke 11:28 NIV*

6. *In the beginning was the Word, and the Word was with God, and the Word was God. John 1:1 NIV*

7. *The Word became flesh and made his dwelling among us. John 1:14a NIV*

NOTES

BLESSING THIRTY-THREE
PROVISION

PRECEPT

The Lord will guide you always; he will satisfy your needs in a sun-scorched land and will strengthen your frame. You will be like a well-watered garden, like a spring whose waters never fall.

Isaiah 58:11 NIV

PRINCIPLE

God wants to provide you with the provision to fulfill His vision for you.

PRACTICE

Many people are confused by how God deals with us regarding supplying us with provision. So many flippantly dismiss the notion that God would care about our financial well being. Some use mocking terms such as "prosperity gospel," rather than carefully examining the concepts behind God's deep desire for us to have full provision to meet all of our needs and to amply supply our purpose.

As effective as mockery is for the simple-minded, it isn't an honest and intellectual argument. Let's not allow ourselves to be robbed of God's Word on the matter, nor rob our children of the benefits of walking in obedience to His Word.

Do you desire that your children have just enough to scrape by, or for them to have more than enough to be amply supplied and able to be generous on every occasion to meet the needs of others? I know the answer before I ask it. You want your children to have more than enough. In fact, it would bring delight to you to know that your children are blessed.

It's not about cars, clothes, and having cottages — it's about a cause and having enough to meet it.

PROFESSION

"My children are designed for a purpose. God made them and He has an assignment for them. God will bring provision into their lives. They are amply supplied to have their needs met and also to meet the needs of others."

PROMISES TO SPEAK THIS WEEK

1. For Scripture says, "Do not muzzle an ox while it is treading out the grain," and "The worker deserves his wages." 1 Timothy 5:18 NIV

2. *Anyone who does not provide for their relatives, and especially for their own household, has denied the faith and is worse than an unbeliever. 1 Timothy 5:8 NIV*

3. *For the blessing of the Lord brings wealth, without painful toil for it. Proverbs 10:22 NIV*

4. *This service that you perform is not only supplying the needs of the Lord's people but is also overflowing in many expressions of thanks to God. 2 Corinthians 9:12 NIV*

5. *You yourselves know that these hands of mine have supplied my own needs and the needs of my companions. Acts 20:34 NIV*

6. *And my God will meet all your needs according to the riches of his glory in Christ Jesus. Philippians 4:19 NIV*

7. *If you, then, though you are evil, know how to give good gifts to your children, how much more will your Father in heaven give good gifts to those who ask him! Matthew 7:11 NIV*

NOTES

BLESSING THIRTY-FOUR
LOVE

PRECEPT

A new command I give you: Love one another. As I have loved you, so you must love one another.

John 13:34 NIV

PRINCIPLE

A life without love is the greatest of all tragedies.

PRACTICE

God is love. He is the personification of love. Therefore, since we are made in the image and likeness of God, love should reflect from us. We want to raise our children in a loving environment. We also want to raise them to know and express love naturally.

There is confusion in our culture that misrepresents love. This culture uses love as a trump card for all kinds of evil and unnatural relationships. Just as God is love, God is also holy. Therefore, love must be holy. If love is not holy, it's actually lust.

We can have all kinds of religious experience, but without love, we're pious without spiritually profiting. We can be the model of philanthropy, but unless we've given in love, our gifts gain no credit. Love isn't hasty or rude. It's not loud and arrogant. Love doesn't dominate or oppress. Love never fails (1 Corinthians 13).

There is a legendary politician from Mobile, Alabama, who would loudly proclaim in his long southern drawl, "Everything's made for love." All the while, his reputation was notoriously ruthless and vile.

We want our children to know what true love is, so that they are not captivated by worthless pursuits of vanity and greed.

PROFESSION

"My children love, and love deeply. They know God's love and then express it with all sincerity in this world. May they have the assurance that they are loved. May they also have the courage to love without measure."

PROMISES TO SPEAK THIS WEEK

1. *...Knowledge puffs up while love builds up. 1 Corinthians 8:1b NIV*

2. *If I speak in the tongues of men and of angels, but do not have love, I am only a resounding gong or a clanging cymbal.*
   1 Corinthians 13:1 NIV

3. If I have a faith that can move mountains, but do not have love, I am nothing. *1 Corinthians 13:2 NIV*

4. If I give all I possess to the poor and give over my body to hardship that I may boast, but do not have love, I gain nothing. *1 Corinthians 13:3 NIV*

5. Love is patient, love is kind. It does not envy, it does not boast, it is not proud. *1 Corinthians 13:4 NIV*

6. Love does not delight in evil but rejoices with the truth. *1 Corinthians 13:6 NIV*

7. Love never fails. *1 Corinthians 13:8a NIV*

NOTES

_____

_____

_____

_____

_____

_____

_____

_____

_____

_____

_____

_____

_____

_____

_____

_____

_____

_____

BLESSING THIRTY-FIVE

A GODLY SPOUSE

PRECEPT

The Lord, before whom I have walked faithfully, will send his angel with you and make your journey a success, so that you can get a wife for my son from my own clans and from my father's family.

Genesis 24:40 NIV

PRINCIPLE

The marriage partner for your child will have a profound influence on your legacy.

PRACTICE

Abraham received his promised son when Isaac was born to him in his old age. Abraham had one more important task before he died — to make sure that Isaac married the kind of woman worthy of Isaac's patriarchal blessing. She would be the bearer of his progeny.

Abraham gives the assignment of finding his son's wife to his butler, the chief servant in his household. Although the servant remains nameless, his assignment is historic. His prayerful diligence to fulfill the task is admirable to say the least. He prayed, *"O Lord, God of my master Abraham, if you will, please grant success to the journey on which I have come"* (Genesis 24:42 NIV).

In fact, this should serve as a lesson for fathers. We should carefully pray for success in the journey of our children marrying the right spouse. The male and female have perfect complementary designs physically. We want them to have perfect complementary designs spiritually, as well.

PROFESSION

"Father, as important as it is for me to raise my children in faith, understanding that their lives are purposed of God, it is equally important for each of their spouses to be raised in the knowledge of Christ, and the hope of their future. Grant my children success in finding the right spouses. Let there be a distinction in the spouses with whom my child will marry. Let them be standouts among their peers, in Jesus' Name. Amen."

PROMISES TO SPEAK THIS WEEK

1. *The Lord God said, "It is not good that the man should be alone. I will make a helper who is just right for him." Genesis 2:18 NLT*

2. ...The people of this age marry and are given in marriage. *Luke 20:34 NIV*

3. ...It is better to marry than to burn with passion. *1 Corinthians 7:9 NIV*

4. ...For this reason a man will leave his father and mother and be united to his wife, and the two will become one flesh. *Matthew 19:5 NIV*

5. He who finds a wife finds what is good and receives favor from the Lord. *Proverbs 18:22 NIV*

6. When Joseph woke up, he did what the angel of the Lord had commanded him and took Mary home as his wife. *Matthew 1:24 NIV*

7. The husband should fulfill his marital duty to his wife, and likewise the wife to her husband. *1 Corinthians 7:3 NIV*

NOTES

_____
_____
_____
_____
_____
_____
_____
_____
_____
_____
_____
_____
_____
_____
_____
_____
_____
_____

BLESSING THIRTY-SIX

LONGEVITY!

★ ★ ★ ★ ★

PRECEPT

"With long life I will satisfy

him and show him

my salvation."

Psalm 91:16 NIV

PRINCIPLE

Longevity upon the earth is a promise for the righteous.

PRACTICE

Is it possible for people to die before their time? Biblically, yes it is. It is not God's will for us to have a shortened lifespan. Tragedy occurs — for which God often receives the blame. You hear foolishness like, "God took them," or "God needed another angel." This kind of irresponsible talk causes a lot of people to blaspheme the character of God. It's slanderous to talk of God "taking people out." He is God the Father, not the Godfather.

We should pray that our children have longevity in life. They should be enabled and empowered to fulfill their days. This is the promise for children who honor their parents, that they will have long and prosperous lives (Ephesians 6:1).

I know you want the best for your children and you want them to have good and fruitful lives. It will take longevity to accomplish their purpose and fulfill their destiny.

PROFESSION

"Father, I speak longevity over my children. I believe they're designed for purpose and to walk in destiny. You know them completely. You fashioned them for a reason. May long life satisfy them, and may they know Your salvation, in Jesus' Name. Amen."

PROMISES TO SPEAK THIS WEEK

1. *Say to him, "Long life to you! Good health to you and your household! And good health to all that is yours!" 1 Samuel 25:6 NIV*

2. *If you walk in obedience to me and keep my decrees and commands as David your father did, I will give you a long life. 1 Kings 3:14 NIV*

3. *With long life I will satisfy him and show him my salvation. Psalm 91:16 NIV*

4.   Long life is in her [wisdom's] right hand; in her left hand are riches and honor. Proverbs 3:16 NIV [Author's comment]

5.   ...It may go well with you and that you may enjoy long life on the earth. Ephesians 6:3

6.   I will sing to the Lord all my life; I will sing praise to my God as long as I live. Psalm 104:33 NIV

7.   Is not wisdom found among the aged? Does not long life bring understanding? Job 12:12 NIV

NOTES

_____

_____

_____

_____

_____

_____

_____

_____

_____

_____

_____

_____

_____

_____

_____

_____

_____

_____

_____

_____

BLESSING THIRTY-SEVEN

CREATIVITY

PRECEPT

No eye has seen, no ear has heard, and no mind has imagined what God has prepared for those who love him.

1 Corinthians 2:9 NLT

PRINCIPLE

God keeps secrets *for* you, not *from* you.

PRACTICE

We're Creationists, meaning, we believe that by Intelligent Design, with incomprehensible wisdom, God created each of us with a specific purpose and intricate details of destiny. He is so masterful in His planning that He withholds the secret wisdom of those details from others and reserves them for us.

With that in mind, you can be sure that your child has God's plans stored within him. *"No one can know a person's thoughts except that person's own spirit, and no one can know God's thoughts except God's own Spirit"* (1 Corinthians 2:11 NLT).

To discover the secret wisdom your children have within them, they'll need to get in touch with their creativity. Their ability and aptitude for ideas, witty inventions, insight, concepts, and imaginations will burst forth from their spirits.

Make no mistake about it, this kind of creativity doesn't come from surface experiences — seeing, hearing, and scheming. No, this secret wisdom is deep. To find it your children will have to dig into the depths of God.

PROFESSION

"Father, I am amazed at my children. I marvel at their ability and creativity. Help me nurture their imagination. Don't allow me to stifle them, but direct them to dig deep in the depths of their spirits. My children need to draw from the secret wisdom that You deposited within them, in Jesus' Name. Amen."

PROMISES TO SPEAK THIS WEEK

1. *No one can know a person's thoughts except that person's own spirit, and no one can know God's thoughts except God's own Spirit. 1 Corinthians 2:11 NLT*

2. People who aren't spiritual can't receive these truths from God's Spirit. 1 Corinthians 2:14a NLT

3. No eye has seen, no ear has heard, and no mind has imagined what God has prepared for those who love him. 1 Corinthians 2:9 NLT

4. I wisdom dwell with prudence, and find out knowledge of witty inventions. Proverbs 8:12 KJV

5. He's filled him with the Spirit of God, with skill, ability, and know-how for making all sorts of things, to design and work in gold, silver, and bronze; to carve stones and set them; to carve wood, working in every kind of skilled craft. Exodus 35:30 MSG

6. He explained to me, "Daniel, I have come here to give you insight and understanding." Daniel 9:22 NLT

7. To these four young men God gave knowledge and understanding of all kinds of literature and learning. And Daniel could understand visions and dreams of all kinds. Daniel 1:17 NIV

NOTES

BLESSING THIRTY-EIGHT

THE BLESSING

PRECEPT

"I will make you into a great nation. I will bless you and make your famous, and you will be a blessing to others."

Genesis 12:2 NLT

PRINCIPLE

We are blessed to be a blessing.

PRACTICE

It's important to discern that *"The Blessing"* is a significant and distinct blessing upon Abraham and his descendants. In order to receive *"The Blessing,"* you would need to be born into the lineage of Abraham, Isaac, and Jacob — the legacy of the promise. The Bible makes it very clear that not all of Abraham's children are included in this special blessing. *"His son by the slave woman was born according to the flesh, but his son by the free woman was born as the result of a divine promise"* (Galatians 4:23 NIV).

The promises were spoken to Abraham and to his seed — not to his seeds — meaning many people. It was spoken to Abraham and to his seed — meaning one person, who is Christ. We need to understand that those who have faith in Jesus, Abraham's seed, are also included in *"The Blessing."*

As fathers, when we speak *"The Blessing"* over our children we are invoking and empowering them to be great, famous, and a blessing to others.

PROFESSION

"My children are children of Abraham through faith in Jesus Christ, therefore, they have 'The Blessing' working on their behalf. My children will be considered great, famous, and a blessing to others!"

PROMISES TO SPEAK THIS WEEK

1. *I will make you into a great nation, and I will bless you; I will make your name great, and you will be a blessing. Genesis 12:2 NIV*

2. *From the Lord comes deliverance. May your blessing be on your people. Psalm 3:8 NIV*

3. *They are always generous and lend freely; their children will be a blessing. Psalm 37:26 NIV*

4.   Your children will be like vigorous young olive trees as they sit around your table. That is the Lord's blessing for those who fear the Him. Psalm 128:3-4 NLT

5.   "The Blessing" of the Lord brings wealth, without painful toll for it. Proverbs 10:22 NIV [Author's emphasis]

6.   I will come in the full measure of "The Blessing" of Christ. Romans 15:29 NIV [Author's emphasis]

7.   He redeemed us in order that "The Blessing" given to Abraham might come to the Gentiles through Christ Jesus, so that by faith we might receive the promise of the Spirit. Galatians 3:14 NIV [Author's emphasis]

NOTES

CHAPTER THIRTY-NINE

FREEDOM!

★ ★ ★ ★ ★

PRECEPT

I will walk about in freedom, for I have sought out your precepts.

Psalm 119:45 NIV

PRINCIPLE

"Freedom is never more than one generation away from extinction." — Ronald Reagan

PRACTICE

It is a cowardly generation that will not fight the foe who will one day enslave their children. As fathers, we have a serious responsibility to stand up for liberty and secure freedom for our children. Unfortunately, this isn't the mantra of the mainstream anymore. There seems to be a growing apathy toward freedom and liberty in a new culture continually surrendering their freedoms for convenience.

We must raise our children to understand the intrinsic value of freedom. The essential nature of freedom for mankind is the original intent for us. Isn't that why Christ came? *"The Spirit of the Lord is upon me, for he has anointed me to bring Good News to the poor. He has sent me to proclaim that captives will be released, that the blind will see, that the oppressed will be set free"* (Luke 4:18 NLT).

Freedom liberates a soul to the opportunity to be what they never could have been under oppression. We must diligently protect this opportunity for our children.

PROFESSION

"Father, malevolent enemies align to take away my children's freedom. The enemies include drug addiction, sexual sins, economic schemes, political maneuverings, etc. Protect my children from these types of captivities. My children will have the opportunity to live out their lives in freedom and to pursue and fulfill their purposes, in Jesus' Name. Amen."

PROMISES TO SPEAK THIS WEEK

1. *...If you can gain your freedom, do so. 1 Corinthians 7:21 NIV*

2. *Now the Lord is the Spirit, and where the Spirit of the Lord is, there is freedom. 2 Corinthians 3:17 NIV*

3. It is for freedom that Christ has set us free. Stand firm, then, and do not let yourselves be burdened again by a yoke of slavery. Galatians 5:1 NIV

4. You, my brothers and sisters, were called to be free. But do not use your freedom to indulge the flesh; rather, serve one another humbly in love. Galatians 5:13 NIV

5. Whoever looks intently into the perfect law that gives freedom, and continues in it — not forgetting what they have heard, but doing it — they will be blessed in what they do. James 1:25 NIV

6. Speak and act as those who are going to be judged by the law that gives freedom. James 2:12 NIV

7. Live as free people.... 1 Peter 2:16 NIV

NOTES

BLESSING FORTY

HEALTH

★ ★ ★ ★ ★

PRECEPT

"...I pray that you may enjoy good health and that all may go well with you, even as your soul is getting along well."

3 John 2 NIV

PRINCIPLE

One of the benefits that comes with knowing God, following His ways, and obeying His precepts is health.

PRACTICE

Health is a big deal. It is becoming a topic of daily discussion. Now that government is getting involved in the minutia of medicine, taking care of one's health is extremely important. You don't want your children at the mercy of health panels.

One of the benefits that comes with following God's ways is health. A huge portion of Jesus' ministry while He was on earth was healing the sick. Obviously, Jesus thought that having a healthy body was a necessity.

I don't know of any parent who would argue that they want their children to be ill or have a disease — nor does God. He wants us to enjoy health.

You would not, and God does not, use sickness to teach your children a lesson. Health is a blessing we speak over our children.

PROFESSION

"I speak the blessing of health over my children. May they always glow with health and be strong to run their race. They need stamina to fulfill their destiny. May they be fit and trim to run with endurance. May they be strong to carry their purpose. May they be quick to correct their course."

PROMISES TO SPEAK THIS WEEK

1. *...Long life to you! Good health to you and your household! And good health to all that is yours! 1 Samuel 25:6*

2. *...Fear the Lord and shun evil. This will bring health to your body and nourishment to your bones. Proverbs 3:8 NIV*

3. *My son, pay attention to what I say; turn your ear to my words... for they are life to those who find them and health to one's whole body. Proverbs 4:20-22 NIV*

4.   *...Good news gives health to the bones. Proverbs 15:30 NIV*

5.   *You restored me to health and let me live. Isaiah 38:16b NIV*

6.   *I will restore you to health and heal your wounds. Jeremiah 30:17a NIV*

7.   *I will bring health and healing to it; I will heal my people and will let them enjoy abundant peace and security. Jeremiah 33:6 NIV*

NOTES

_____

_____

_____

_____

_____

_____

_____

_____

_____

_____

_____

_____

_____

_____

_____

_____

_____

_____

_____

_____

_____

BLESSING FORTY-ONE

PEACE

PRECEPT

The Lord turn his face

toward you and

give you peace.

Numbers 6:26 NIV

PRINCIPLE

Peace secures a person in calm assurance, even in the midst of storms.

PRACTICE

There is an epidemic that has invaded our children's lives called Attention Deficit Hyperactive Disorder (ADHD). Another enemy that has surfaced is the prevalence of childhood depression. The only solution that many feel useful is prescription drugs. I am not against medicine and will not argue against the need for these drugs; however, I want to encourage you that speaking a blessing of peace over your child will certainly help with these matters.

You want your child to be at peace. Peace will give your child a calmness that surpasses their circumstances. Regardless of the challenges they may face, they can have an assurance that no matter what happens, they are at peace.

When the Lord turns his face toward your children, they will receive a peace that passes understanding.

PROFESSION

"Father, my children will be taught of the Lord, and great will be the peace of my children. Even in the midst of storms, my children will have calm assurance. During troubling times, they will have a confidence that You are their protector and the provider of peace, in Jesus' Name. Amen."

PROMISES TO SPEAK THIS WEEK

1. *All your children will be taught by the Lord, and great will be their peace. Isaiah 54:13 NIV*

2. *In peace I will lie down and sleep, for you alone, Lord, make me dwell in safety. Psalm 4:8 NIV*

3. *The Lord gives strength to his people; the Lord blesses his people with peace. Psalm 29:11 NIV*

4. *Turn from evil and do good; seek peace and pursue it. Psalm 34:14 NIV*

5. *Consider the blameless, observe the upright; a future awaits those who seek peace. Psalm 37:37 NIV*

6. *Love and faithfulness meet together, righteousness and peace kiss each other. Psalm 85:10 NIV*

7. *A heart at peace gives life to the body. Proverbs 14:30a NIV*

NOTES

_____

_____

_____

_____

_____

_____

_____

_____

_____

_____

_____

_____

_____

_____

_____

_____

_____

_____

_____

_____

BLESSING FORTY-TWO

WEALTH

PRECEPT

The man became rich, and his wealth continued to grow until he became very wealthy.

Genesis 26:13 NIV

PRINCIPLE

The wealth that God brings into your life is a blessing.

PRACTICE

If we're not careful, we can buy into the popular notion that wealth creation can only happen if you're doing something evil. There are men who do evil and profit from it — drug dealers, sex traffickers, porn peddlers, men who manipulate currencies and charge usury — but, if we live a righteous life, those people will never make a dime off of us.

In the Bible, wealth accumulation is demonstrated in examples of those who feared God and walked according to His ways. In fact, it is recognized as such a direct link to His blessing upon a person's life that we're warned not to take personal credit for our wealth. *"He did all this so you would never say to yourself, 'I have achieved this wealth with my own strength and energy'"* (Deuteronomy 8:17 NLT).

We are admonished to remember the Lord, for it is He who gives us the ability to produce wealth (Deuteronomy 8:18). When we remember that God is the one who empowers us to produce, then greed or pride in wealth is a non-issue. I've known wealthy people who were anti-prosperity because they didn't want to give God the credit for their wealth. They claimed that it all came from their hard work and ingenious abilities. That's foolish and destructive. Pride comes before a fall.

Let's speak the blessing of wealth over our children to recognize that God will give them the ability to produce and accumulate wealth. When God brings them wealth, He will add no trouble with it.

PROFESSION

"Father, I know that You are the One who sends wealth. You humble and You exalt. I pray that my children will be producers of wealth and will remember You in it. I know that wealth isn't evil; however, it can reveal an evil heart or intentions, so bless my children to be wealthy, and remind them to always acknowledge You, in Jesus' Name. Amen."

PROMISES TO SPEAK THIS WEEK

1. *Remember the Lord your God, for it is he who gives you the ability to produce wealth, and so confirms his covenant, which he swore to your ancestors, as it is today. Deuteronomy 8:18 NIV*

2. *All the wealth God has given you from our father legally belongs to us and our children. So go ahead and do whatever God has told you. Genesis 31:16 NLT*

3. *Return to your homes with your great wealth — with large herds of livestock, with silver, gold, bronze, and iron, and a great quantity of clothing…. Joshua 22:8 NIV*

4. *Moreover, I will give you what you have not asked for — both wealth and honor — so that in your lifetime you will have no equal among kings. 1 Kings 3:13 NIV*

5. *Wealth and riches are in their houses, and their righteousness endures forever. Psalm 112:3 NIV*

6. *Honor the Lord with your wealth, with the firstfruits of all your crops. Proverbs 3:9 NIV*

7. *The blessing of the Lord brings wealth, without painful toil for it. Proverbs 10:22 NIV*

NOTES

_____

_____

_____

_____

_____

_____

_____

_____

_____

_____

WORSHIP WITH GRATITUDE

PRECEPT

Yes, they knew God, but they wouldn't worship him as God or even give him thanks. And they began to think up foolish ideas of what God was like. As a result, their minds became dark and confused.

Romans 1:21 NLT

PRINCIPLE

Gratitude is a key for your children to have a sound mind. Worship is the expression of gratitude toward God.

PRACTICE

It is extremely important to raise children with a heart of gratitude and the ability to express that gratitude toward whoever has given them favor or a gift.

Gratitude is a conscious acknowledgement of a benefit received. When children are raised to express gratitude, you will see tremendous blessings flow into their lives. Gratitude is truly a key for the favor of God and man to work on their behalf.

On the contrary, children who aren't grateful stop the flow of favor in their lives and begin to have confusion in their minds.

Paul gave us this warning by pointing to those who had the knowledge of God but neither worshipped nor thanked Him. These ungrateful people became perverted in their thinking, changing the course of their natural desires. They began to worship what they crafted with their own hands and to lust for unnatural affections. Amazingly, this happened because they were not grateful. Showing gratitude is vital.

As fathers, we should model worship and a heart of gratitude toward God. This will show our children that, even as adults, we show humility toward God by expressing our gratitude.

PROFESSION

"Father, I am so grateful for all you've done for me. You've blessed me with my family. I want to worship You and express my appreciation for Your kindness toward me. I want to raise my children with this same heart of gratitude and worship. Help my children have a heart that expresses their love for You. Let your Spirit awaken their hearts, in Jesus' Name. Amen."

PROMISES

1. *Give thanks to the Lord, for he is good! His faithful love endures forever. 1 Chronicles 16:34 NLT*

2. *I will thank the Lord because he is just; I will sing praise to the name of the Lord Most High. Psalm 7:17 NLT*

3. *I will give thanks to you, Lord, with all my heart; I will tell of all your wonderful deeds. Psalm 9:1 NIV*

4. *Is not the cup of thanksgiving for which we give thanks a participation in the blood of Christ? And is not the bread that we break a participation in the body of Christ? 1 Corinthians 10:16 NIV*

5. *Be thankful in all circumstances, for this is God's will for you who belong to Christ Jesus. 1 Thessalonians 5:18 NLT*

6. *Now, our God, we give you thanks, and praise your glorious name. 1 Chronicles 29:13 NIV*

7. *I will give you thanks, for you answered me; you have become my salvation. Psalm 118:21 NIV*

NOTES

BLESSING FORTY-FOUR

A SOUND MIND!

★ ★ ★ ★ ★

PRECEPT

When doubts filled my mind, your comfort gave me renewed hope and cheer.

Psalm 94:19 NLT

PRINCIPLE

A person cannot rise above their belief system.

PRACTICE

As fathers, it's our responsibility to teach our children their belief systems. I know that conflicts with many people's ideas concerning parenting. Some think we shouldn't impose, or even instruct, our children in their faith. I find the concept appalling and irrational — it doesn't make any sense if you would apply that to other areas of life.

If you knew how to manage money extremely well and were able to turn ideas into enormous wealth, wouldn't you share that knowledge with your children? If you were a doctor and your child was suffering from sickness, wouldn't you prescribe the antidote to give your child comfort and restore them to health? Likewise, if you have a belief system in Christ Jesus — a personal faith that gives you eternal life — don't you think you should instruct your children in that faith?

Teaching your children the Bible gives them hope. It gives them the ability to think differently — literally, giving them a sound mind. I am confident that you want your children to enjoy life and have a hope for their future.

Don't pawn this off on the local church or someone else. Take the initiative and teach your children what you know and what you learn from God's Word.

PROFESSION

"I know how to teach my children the Word of God, so they have the kind of thinking that gives them hope and lets them enjoy life. I may not be a seasoned teacher, but God will instruct me on what I should say to my children. They have sound minds, according to the Word of God."

PROMISES TO SPEAK THIS WEEK

1. ..."Who has known the mind of the Lord so as to instruct him?" But we have the mind of Christ. 1 Corinthians 2:16 NIV

2. We destroy arguments and every lofty opinion raised against the knowledge of God, and take every thought captive to obey Christ. 2 Corinthians 10:5 ESV

3. Having hope will give you courage. You will be protected and will rest in safety. Job 11:18 NLT

4. May integrity and uprightness preserve me, for I wait for you. Psalm 25:21 ESV

5. Oh, what joy for those whose disobedience is forgiven, whose sin is put out of sight! Psalm 32:1 NLT

6. What joy for those who can live in your house, always singing your praises. Psalm 84:4 NLT

7. For the word of God is alive and powerful. It is sharper than the sharpest two-edged sword, cutting between soul and spirit, between joint and marrow. It exposes our innermost thoughts and desires. Hebrews 4:12 NLT

NOTES

BLESSING FORTY-FIVE

GENERATIONAL BLESSING!

PRECEPT

I'll make them of one mind and heart, always honoring me, so that they can live good and whole lives, they and their children after them.

Jeremiah 32:39 MSG

PRINCIPLE

God wants you to establish directional intent for generations.

PRACTICE

Let's be honest. As men, we're motivated to work long and grueling hours so that we can make a better life for our children above what we inherited. Most of us have come from small beginnings. Yet, as we live out our days, there is an internal drive (at *FivestarMan,* we call it an entrepreneurial drive) to meet our needs, to grant the desires of our family, and to finance our purpose.

God speaks of gathering scattered people back into the land that He swore to their ancestry, namely, Israel. He said He would make them have one mind and heart, or one purpose. His desire is for them to live good and whole lives. He also wants the generations that follow to have the same promise. This literally is a generational blessing.

Do you know you can give your family intentional direction to live honorable lives — living in complete unity of your mind and purpose — so they can have good and whole lives?

That's really what these 52 blessings for you to speak over your children are. They are empowering your children to be of one heart and purpose with you. Your children will know you have the very best in mind for them. They'll never question your heart. They'll know you've done your best to give them a better life than what you've had.

PROFESSION

"Father, my goal today is to bless my progeny, the generations that follow me. I want at least three generations removed from me to know I honored Your name and served You well. Now, I speak over my children, and command them in the ways of God. I want them to live good and whole lives, in Jesus' Name. Amen."

PROMISES TO SPEAK THIS WEEK

1. *Let all that I am praise the Lord; may I never forget the good things he does for me. Psalm 103:2 NLT*

2. For he satisfies the thirsty and fills the hungry with good things. Psalm 107:9 NLT

3. They themselves will be wealthy, and their good deeds will last forever. Psalm 112:3 NLT

4. O Lord, do good to those who are good, whose hearts are in tune with you. Psalm 125:4 NLT

5. Do not withhold good from those who deserve it when it's in your power to help them. Proverbs 3:27 NLT

6. My child, listen to me and do as I say, and you will have a long, good life. Proverbs 4:10

7. Follow the steps of good men instead, and stay on the paths of the righteous. Proverbs 2:20 NLT

NOTES

GODLY FEAR
VERSUS DEADLY FEAR

PRECEPT

*For God has not given us
a spirit of fear and
timidity, but of power,
love, and self-discipline.*

2 Timothy 1:7 NLT

PRINCIPLE

When you fear God you won't fear anything else.

PRACTICE

The Biblical term for fear can be confusing. To fear God is to reverence and be in awe of Him and His power. It is humbly knowing your place and showing respectful admiration for who He is. Prophets who spoke with God often fell down as if they had died. Think about that! They fell as dead men.

That's a far cry from the arrogant and flippant attitudes that some people bloviate toward God Almighty. They show no fear of Him. To be honest, that's ignorant and overwhelmingly stupid.

On the other hand, we don't want our children be controlled by fear or to be timid about life and paralyzed by insecurities.

My daughter-in-law asked my son, "What did your parents do to make you and your siblings so confident to try new things? How did they raise you to be so adventurous and assured?"

My wife and I talked about it and concluded their confidence came from one primary thing: Every day, on the way to school, we all made a confession of faith saying, "I can do all things through Christ who strengthens me" (Philippians 4:13 NKJV).

There could be other things that contributed to their strong belief and fearless attitude, but this is the most important one. When you speak God's promises over your children, they become part of their thinking, and their natural reaction is so contrary to their peers that people will take notice.

PROFESSION

"My children will not fear man or disasters or plagues or taking bold risks in their life. They won't be afraid of the dark because God is their light. They won't fear their friends or fear peer pressure because they're insecure. They will fear God. They will have complete reverence and respect toward Him."

PROMISES TO SPEAK THIS WEEK

1. For the angel of the Lord is a guard; he surrounds and defends all who fear him. Psalm 34:7 NLT

2. Fear the Lord, you his godly people, for those who fear him will have all they need. Psalm 34:9 NLT

3. Come, my children, and listen to me, and I will teach you to fear the Lord. Psalm 34:11 NLT

4. God is our refuge and strength, always ready to help in times of trouble. So we will not fear when earthquakes come and the mountains crumble into the sea. Psalm 46:1-2 NLT

5. Why should I fear when trouble comes, when enemies surround me? Psalm 49:5 NLT

6. Fear of the Lord is the foundation of true wisdom. All who obey his commandments will grow in wisdom. Praise him forever! Psalm 111:10-11 NLT

7. The Lord is for me, so I will have no fear. What can mere people do to me? Psalm 118:6 NLT

NOTES

_____
_____
_____
_____
_____
_____
_____
_____
_____
_____
_____
_____
_____

COMPASSION FOR THE NEEDY

PRECEPT

The Lord is good to everyone. He showers compassion on all his creation.

Psalm 145:9 NLT

PRINCIPLE

Raise compassionate children who are moved by the needs of others.

PRACTICE

The Hebrew word for **compassion** gives us the picture of someone whose entrails are convulsing with movement. It represents the seat of emotions being moved with sympathy toward another. That's a picture of God who looks down at mankind and is moved with compassion; the seat of His emotions move Him.

You see this represented by Jesus when a man with leprosy came and knelt in front of Him, begging to be healed. *"If you are willing, you can heal me and make me clean,"* he said. The Bible says that Jesus was moved with compassion and healed him (Mark 1:41).

Recently, a father approached me and shared how he asked his son to help him with one of the *FivestarMan 45-Day Challenges.* His challenge was to gather all of his loose change and give it to someone in need — "to gather the fragments and let nothing be wasted" (Mark 6:43). As he and his son were driving to a ballgame, he asked his son, "Help me find someone in need. I have some money that I've gathered to give to them." This man teared up telling me how this one challenge changed his relationship with his son. He said, "We connected on a deep level by giving a homeless man some money. When my son handed the needy man some money, I saw manhood arise within him."

Expose your children to the needs of others and show them how they can help with a compassionate heart.

PROFESSION

"Father, I don't want my children to go through life with blinders on. I want them to be very aware of their surroundings, with their eyes open to the needs of this world. I pray for my children to have and show compassion to those who are hurting, to be like Christ who was moved with compassion for those in need, in Jesus' Name. Amen."

PROMISES TO SPEAK THIS WEEK

1.   Have compassion on me, Lord, for I am weak. Psalm 6:2a NLT

2.   ...Let your compassion quickly meet our needs.... Psalm 79:8 NLT

3.   For the Lord will give justice to his people and have compassion on his servants. Psalm 135:14 NLT

4.   The Lord is good to everyone. He showers compassion on all his creation. Psalm 145:9 NLT

5.   When he saw the crowds, he had compassion on them because they were confused and helpless, like sheep without a shepherd. Matthew 9:36 NLT

6.   Moved with compassion, Jesus reached out and touched him. "I am willing," he said. "Be healed!" Mark 1:41 NLT

7.   God knows how much I love you and long for you with the tender compassion of Christ Jesus. Philippians 1:8 NLT

NOTES

BLESSING FORTY-EIGHT
MATURITY

PRECEPT

When I was a child, I spoke like a child, I thought like a child, I reasoned like a child. When I became a man, I gave up childish ways.

1 Corinthians 13:11 ESV

PRINCIPLE

The goal of parenting is to teach children to make mature decisions.

PRACTICE

We're facing a parenting crisis in our culture. More and more children are being raised without proper parenting and oversight by mature adults. We know the epidemic of fatherless homes. The collateral damage is a society of childish thinking in those who should be adults.

A child becomes an adult when they put away childish thinking. It's an incredible thrill when you see your child make a calculated and wise decision. There is a sense of pride that is refreshing to see them step into maturity.

Not long ago, I saw my son navigate a very difficult decision concerning his business relationship with a company. As much as he enjoyed the comforts and privileges that came with that company, he knew that it was not a good fit for the long-term. I prayed with him and asked God to give him wisdom and discernment regarding his decision. Within the next few days, I saw him make decisions that seemed amazingly mature for his age. I was so proud of him. He didn't ask me to make the decisions. He simply asked me to pray with him about his decisions.

PROFESSION

"Father, You've given me the responsibility to teach and train my children to make wise and calculated decisions. I need You to help me direct them toward maturity. Give me insight, understanding, and long-term thinking regarding their lives, in Jesus' Name. Amen."

PROMISES TO SPEAK THIS WEEK

1. *John grew up and became strong in spirit. And he lived in the wilderness until he began his public ministry to Israel. Luke 1:80 NLT*

2. There the child grew up healthy and strong. He was filled with wisdom, and God's favor was on him. Luke 2:40 NLT

3. Jesus grew in wisdom and in stature and in favor with God and all the people. Luke 2:52 NLT

4. It was by faith that Moses, when he grew up, refused to be called the son of Pharaoh's daughter. Hebrews 11:24 NLT

5. When I was a child, I spoke and thought and reasoned as a child. But when I grew up, I put away childish things. 1 Corinthians 13:11 NLT

6. Solid food is for those who are mature, who through training have the skill to recognize the difference between right and wrong. Hebrews 5:14 NLT

7. We are glad to seem weak if it helps show that you are actually strong. We pray that you will become mature. 2 Corinthians 13:9 NLT

NOTES

BLESSING FORTY-NINE
CHOSEN

★ ★ ★ ★ ★

PRECEPT

...You children of his servant Abraham, you descendants of Jacob, his chosen ones.

Psalm 105:6 NLT

PRINCIPLE

There comes a time when you must relate to your children as brothers and sisters in Christ, rather than simply as your children.

PRACTICE

My friend Ken Blount shared with me this powerful principle. He said, "Neil, your children are young, but they won't always be young. As they get older, you'll need to adjust your relationship with them. You'll need to relate to your children as brothers and sisters in Christ, not just as your children."

I must admit that at the time it was a difficult concept to grasp. How do I relate to them as a brother or sister?

I saw in the scripture that Abraham related to his wife, Sarah, not only as his wife, but as his sister for he said, "She really is my sister, for we both have the same father, but different mothers. And I married her." Interestingly, Abraham was related to Sarah both as a husband and as a brother. They shared the same father but different mothers.

In the case of our children, we can relate to God as Father equally because God is not their grandfather, but He has chosen them and He is their Father. Therefore, as they get older we can have the unique relationship that they are also our brothers and sisters in Christ.

PROFESSION

"Father, help me see my children's relationship with You is one that You've chosen. You have a direct relationship with my children. You are their Heavenly Father. They're your children, in Jesus' Name. Amen."

PROMISES TO SPEAK THIS WEEK

1. *Do not touch my chosen people, and do not hurt my prophets. 1 Chronicles 16:22*

2. *Look at my servant, whom I strengthen. He is my chosen one, who pleases me. I have put my Spirit upon him.... Isaiah 42:1 NLT*

3. *You went out to rescue your chosen people, to save your anointed ones. Habakkuk 3:13a NLT*

4. *We know, dear brothers and sisters, that God loves you and has chosen you to be his own people. 1 Thessalonians 1:4 NLT*

5. *…You are a chosen people. You are royal priests, a holy nation, God's very own possession. 1 Peter 2:9 NLT*

6. *Then they all prayed, "O Lord, you know every heart. Show us which of these men you have chosen." Acts 1:24 NLT*

7. *That is why Christ did not honor himself by assuming he could become High Priest. No, he was chosen by God, who said to him, "You are my Son. Today I have become your Father." Hebrews 5:5 NLT*

NOTES

REVELATION

PRECEPT

Where there is no revelation, people cast off restraint; but blessed is the one who heeds wisdom's instruction.

Proverbs 29:18 NIV

PRINCIPLE

Children need revelation to give them directional intent for their life.

PRACTICE

This could be one of the most important blessings to speak over your children. **Revelation** is a unique word that means **an oracle.** An oracle can be a word, a picture, or even a person who gives authoritative and wise answers.

Solomon said that where there is no revelation, people cast off restraint.

You've seen young people who had no restraint. Haven't you wondered, "Where are their parents?" Or maybe, you've said, "If that were my kid…" You recognize those children do not have a revelation. They are subject to stupidity — constantly making dumb decisions.

You want your children to have revelation. It gives them a picture to pursue in life. It sets a goal for them and keeps them on track. It puts curbs in their lives that will keep them out of the ditch.

PROFESSION

"Father, my children need to hear a word from You. They need to have a revelation that will help guide them in the right direction. I pray that as they mature, their lives will be guarded by revelation. Give them a glimpse into the future to see how the decisions they make today determine their destiny, in Jesus' Name. Amen."

PROMISES TO SPEAK THIS WEEK

1. *When there is a prophet among you, I, the Lord, reveal myself to them in visions, I speak to them in dreams. Numbers 12:6 NIV*

2. *Day after day they pour forth speech; night after night they reveal knowledge. Psalm 19:2 NIV*

3. *Yes, there are great benefits! First of all, the Jews were entrusted with the whole revelation of God. Romans 3:2 NLT*

4. *I received my message from no human source, and no one taught me. Instead, I received it by direct revelation from Jesus Christ. Galatians 1:12 NIV*

5. *I keep asking that the God of our Lord Jesus Christ, the glorious Father, may give you the Spirit of wisdom and revelation, so that you may know him better. Ephesians 1:17 NIV*

6. *I pray that the eyes of your heart may be enlightened in order that you may know the hope to which he has called you, the riches of his glorious inheritance in his holy people. Ephesians 1:18 NIV*

7. *The revelation from Jesus Christ, which God gave him to show his servants what must soon take place... Revelation 1:1 NIV*

NOTES

_____

_____

_____

_____

_____

_____

_____

_____

_____

_____

_____

_____

_____

_____

_____

_____

_____

_____

SPIRITUAL WEAPONS

PRECEPT

The weapons we fight with are not the weapons of the world. On the contrary, they have divine power to demolish strongholds.

2 Corinthians 10:4 NIV

PRINCIPLE

Don't leave your children defenseless.

PRACTICE

My wife began a practice each day. While driving our children to school, she would lead them in this confession:

Today, we put on the full armor of God,
The helmet of salvation,
The breastplate of righteousness,
The belt of truth.
Our feet are shod with the preparation of the Gospel of peace.
We have the sword of the Spirit,
The shield of faith.
We're ready to face the day, in Jesus' Name.
I can do all things through Christ who strengthens me.

She would also add:

My children are taught of the Lord.
Great is their peace and undisturbed composure.
They have the mind of Christ, and excel in everything
They put their hands to do.

I can't tell you what this did to shape the course of their lives. I believe it was pivotal and still works on their behalf. Recently, my daughter-in-law shared with us that my son speaks this over her as she is leaving the house.

My children will never forget this confession. It is imprinted in their DNA. When your children hear you speak these blessings over them, it will be revolutionary in their character and personal confidence.

PROFESSION

"Father, my children are not unarmed. They have the weapons of supernatural ability to demolish every false spirit and lie of the enemy. They're not defenseless. They are well armed and able to fight the good fight of faith, in Jesus' Name. Amen."

PROMISES TO SPEAK THIS WEEK

1. *He put on righteousness as his breastplate, and the helmet of salvation on his head; he put on the garments of vengeance and wrapped himself in zeal as in a cloak. Isaiah 59:17 NIV*

2. *Therefore put on the full armor of God, so that when the day of evil comes, you may be able to stand your ground, and after you have done everything, to stand. Ephesians 6:13 NIV*

3. *But since we belong to the day, let us be sober, putting on faith and love as a breastplate, and the hope of salvation as a helmet. 1 Thessalonians 5:8 NIV*

4. *Deliver me from the sword, my precious life from the power of the dogs. Psalm 22:20 NIV*

5. *Gird your sword on your side, you mighty one; clothe yourself with splendor and majesty. Psalm 45:3 NIV*

6. *Don't let evil conquer you, but conquer evil by doing good. Romans 12:21 NLT*

7. *For everyone born of God overcomes the world. This is the victory that has overcome the world, even our faith. 1 John 5:4 NIV*

NOTES

BLESSING FIFTY-TWO

LEGACY

★ ★ ★ ★ ★

PRECEPT

Good people leave an inheritance to their grandchildren, but the sinner's wealth passes to the godly.

Proverbs 13:22 NLT

PRINCIPLE

A man of real faith believes for something that requires longer than his own lifetime to come true.

PRACTICE

Solomon made this interesting observation: *"God has put eternity into man's heart"* (Ecclesiastes 3:11).

In the last season of man's lifetime, he sits on the porch and conducts an audit of his life. He surveys the recesses of his life's path. He thinks about the things that cluttered his life. He pushes aside the cars, clothes, and cottages, and wonders, "Did I do anything that I will be remembered for?"

I have reached the place of life that I've surveyed what matters most to me. I live to hear one compliment. It motivates me. In inspires me. It controls my appetite. It crucifies my flesh. It is to hear my children tell their children, "We serve the God of my father."

I want to leave a legacy for those who will follow me
A godly inheritance for those who will bear my name
And when I leave time behind and stories are told of me
More than the 'good old times'
I pray it's a legacy
— Tim Simmons, lyrics of "Legacy"

PROFESSION

*"Father, I want to leave a legacy. I have prayed for 52 weeks 'The Blessing' over my children. I continually bring them before You. I only have a short window of time to impact their lives and influence their destiny. Help me be **the man,** the father that they need. I speak blessing over their lives, in Jesus' Name. Amen."*

PROMISES TO SPEAK THIS WEEK

1. *And in all the land were no women found so fair as the daughters of Job: and their father gave them inheritance among their brethren. Job 42:15 KJV*

2. Ask of me, and I shall give thee the heathen for thine inheritance, and the uttermost parts of the earth for thy possession. *Psalm 2:8 KJV*

3. Save your people and bless your inheritance; be their shepherd and carry them forever. *Psalm 28:9 NIV*

4. For the Lord will not reject his people; he will never forsake his inheritance. *Psalm 94:14 NIV*

5. I walk in the way of righteousness, along the paths of justice, bestowing a rich inheritance on those who love me and making their treasuries full. *Proverbs 8:20-21 NIV*

6. By faith Abraham, when called to go to a place he would later receive as his inheritance, obeyed and went, even though he did not know where he was going. *Hebrews 11:8 NIV*

7. ...In his great mercy he has given us new birth into a living hope through the resurrection of Jesus Christ from the dead and into an inheritance that can never perish, spoil or fade. This inheritance is kept in heaven for you. *1 Peter 1:3-4 NIV*

NOTES

CONCLUSION

FAITH FOR THE FUTURE

As fathers, we do not know what the future holds for our children. We don't know exactly what challenges they will face. As we see culture's morals, ethics, and values continue to slide into wickedness, we can be troubled. How will our children fare in this world?

"We cannot always build the future for our youth, but we can build our youth for the future." — Franklin D. Roosevelt

For 52 weeks, you've confessed these blessings over your children. You've activated your faith by declaring from your own mouth the promises of God. Now, we must have confidence that God will watch over His Word to perform it in the lives of our children. Our confidence is based upon the flawless character of our Father. He is not a man that He can lie. He isn't flippant with His promises.

I want to encourage you to keep this book handy. Keep it near you. Regularly return to it — pick it up and rehearse the promises. I would go so far as to say, continue to use it daily for as long as your children are in your home. My wife, Kay, and I continue to pray and confess promises on behalf of our children — and now, for our grandchildren.

It is important for me to say this in closing — it's very easy to allow regret to enter into your spirit. Especially as we get older and wiser, we look back and sigh, "If I had only known then..." Well, nostalgia is an obsession for an unattainable past. We can't go back and do it over. Life doesn't give us mulligans. Life is a process of growth. We have the right to grow, mature and become wiser.

If you've failed as a father, welcome to the club — we all have — however, I've found that forgiveness is easier when it is spoken.

I've shared my story and have been transparent regarding my father leaving our family when I was only five years of age. I didn't know him until I became a young man. By that time, he had moved on and raised his wife's five children. When we reconnected, I had become a believer in Christ. I remember the day that we sat down in the booth of a hamburger dive in a small town in Oklahoma. At first the conversation was awkward, difficult and distant.

As I looked across the table to see a man I really didn't know who was my father, I began to calculate how old he was when he walked out the door of our lives to start a new life. He was a young man in his late twenties. In the year of 1966, he lost his father to cancer. His mother died. He lost his job as an executive at General Electric Corporation, and his wife committed adultery — all in one year.

Wow! I looked across the table and suddenly related to him as a young man. I had a difficult year, but nothing compared to that. I realized the pain. I felt the knot in my stomach. Compassion flooded my spirit.

I said, "I want you to know, I forgive you. For the rest of my life I will relate to you as your son. I will honor you as my father. Don't hold this against yourself."

You may have a similar story or even one worse than mine. My hope is that you don't allow your past to determine your future. Don't allow the iniquities of your father to be passed on to your children. Stop the tragedy in your time.

> *Jabez cried out to the God of Israel, "Oh, that you would bless me and enlarge my territory! Let your hand be with me, and keep me from harm so that I will be free from pain." And God granted his request.*
>
> *1 Chronicles 4:10 NIV*

Stuck in the middle of a biblical genealogy is this amazing verse. In the midst of the routine of the "begets" comes a young man literally named "Pain" in the Hebrew language. Yet, within him was the deep-seated purpose of being gallant. Jabez was more honorable than his brothers. When Jabez cried out to God, "Keep me from harm so that I will be free from pain," he changed his bloodline from a curse into a blessing.

The "begets" that follow may not have known their ancestry. They may not have realized the advantages they enjoyed because of their father, grandfather, or great-grandfather, named, Pain. They may not have grasped the significance of his prayer, but they enjoyed the benefits of it.

Your descendants may not know when, where, and with whom the advantages of their life were birthed. They may not put the credit to your name, but that's all right. That's not why you've been faithful to make these confessions of faith.

What's important is that you lifted your eyes toward Heaven, raised your deep baritone voice to your Heavenly Father, stretched forth your hands and declared *"The Blessing"* upon your children.

With that, all I can add is... Amen, and so be it!

— *Neil Kennedy*

ABOUT THE AUTHOR

NEIL KENNEDY

Neil Kennedy is the founder of FivestarMan, an international movement for men. Neil has authored several books, including *FivestarMan: The Five Passions Of Authentic Manhood, The Centurion Principle, A Mother's Guide To Raising A FivestarMan, God's Currency, Seven Laws Which Govern Increase And Order,* and *Speaking The Father's Blessing.*

Neil is also a sought-after contributor to many publications, authoring multiple articles for journals and national magazines, and he publishes the popular **"Daily Champion"** for men.

CONTACT
INFORMATION

To contact the author or to obtain more information

Please Contact:

Neil Kennedy

FivestarMan

402B W. Mount Vernon St., Box 333

Nixa, MO 65714

★ ★ ★ ★ ★

To obtain information on
hosting a FivestarMan Event, visit:

FivestarMan.com

Made in the USA
Charleston, SC
29 October 2015